Geography Matters

SCOTLAND 1

Series Editor:

John Hopkin

Editor:

Philip Duffy

Authors:

Heather Blades, Deepings School, Peterborough
Sue Lomas, Henbury High School, Macclesfield
Chris Ryan, formerly at Heston Community School, London
Linda Thompson, formerly at Sandbach School, Sandbach
Paul Thompson, Dunsdale High School, Wolverhampton

Heinemann

Heinemann Educational Publishers
Halley Court, Jordan Hill, Oxford, OX2 8EJ
a division of Reed Educational & Professional Publishing Ltd
Heinemann is a registered trademark of Reed Educational & Professional Publishing Ltd

OXFORD MELBOURNE AUCKLAND
JOHANNESBURG BLANTYRE GABORONE
IBADAN PORTSMOUTH NH (USA) CHICAGO

First published 2002

ISBN 0 435 35543 0

06 05 04 03 02 01

10 9 8 7 6 5 4 3 2 1

Edited by Caroline Hannan

Designed, produced and illustrated by Gecko Ltd, Bicester, Oxon
Illustrated by Peter Ball, Inkwell, Dave Mostyn, Roger Penwill, Chris Rothero, John Storey, Tokay, Geoff Ward and Tony Wilkins

Original illustrations © Heinemann Educational Publishers 2002

Printed and bound in Spain by Edelvives

Acknowledgements
The authors and publishers would like to thank the following for permission to reproduce copyright material.

Photos
p. 4 Corbis /Craig Aurness, Yann Arthus-Bertrand, Catherine Karnow; *D* © Phil Duffy; *E* Corbis/Galen Rowell; *F* The Stock Market. **p. 5** *A–C* Corbis/Paul A.Souders, Vince Streano. **pp. 6, 7** *C, D* Science Photo Library/M-Sat Ltd **p. 8** *A* SPL/Tom Van Sant/ Geosphere Project/Planetary Visions. **p. 10** *A* Dave Marriott. **p. 14** *F* Corbis/Owen Franken; **p. 20** *A*, Associated Press; *B* Corbis/AFP; *C* Corbis/Nik Wheeler; *D* Associated Press. **p. 21** *E* Corbis/AFP; *F* Associated Press; *G* Corbis/George Hall; *H* Associated Press; *I* Rex Features/Sipa Press; *J* Rex Features/Sipa Press. **p. 25** *A* GeoScience Features Picture Library. **p. 26** *A*, B Dr. Jurg Alean. **p. 29** *C* Corbis/Bettmann; *D* Rex Features/Sipa Press; *E* R.P. Hoblitt, US Geological Survey. **p. 30** *G* Corbis/Yann Arthus-Bertrand; *H* Rex Features/Sipa Press. **p. 31** *L* Tokai University Research & Information Center (TRIC); *M* Corbis/Paul A. Souders. **p. 33** *E*, Ref from BBC website: www.bbc.co.uk/search Popperfoto/Reuters; *F* Rex Features/Sipa press. **p. 36** *A, B* Rex Features/Sipa Press; *C* Corbis/Joseph Sohm; *D* Corbis/AFP; *E, F* Associated Press. **pp. 37, 38** *D*, **39** *E*, **40** *J* Rex Features/Sipa Press. **p. 40** *K* Corbis/AFP; *L* Rex Features/Sipa Press. **p. 41** *N* Corbis/AFP. **p. 42** *A* Corbis/Craig Lovell; *B* Earthquake Hazard Centre/Rajendra Desai. **p. 43** *E, F* SPL/ David Parker. **p. 45** *C* Image bank/Getty Images. **p. 46** *B* U.S. Agency for International Development/Miami-Dade Fire Rescue Squad. **p. 48** *A* SPL; *B* James Davis Worldwide; *C* Corbis/Michael S. Yamashita. **p. 50** *A* Stock Market/Tibor Bognar; *B* SPL/Earth Satellite Corp; *C* Corbis; *D* © Mike Ridout; *E* Yann Arthus-bertrand. **p. 51** *J* FLPA/Fritz Pölking; *F* Corbis/Yann Arthus-Bertrand; *G* PA Photos/ Owen Humphreys; *H* Stock Market; **p. 52, 53** *A* Skyscan/A Sanger-Davies; *B* © Alan Bilham-Boult. **p. 56** *A* © Heather Blades. **p. 57** *A* John & Eliza Forder; **p. 64** *B* PA Photos/John Giles; **p. 65** *C* © John Hopkin. **p. 66** *A* Scottish Viewpoint; *B* Stock Market/Jose Fuste Rago; *C, D* Stock Market; *E* Scottish Highland Photo Library. **p. 68** *A* © Sue Anderson; *B* Stock Market; *C* FLPA/Peter Reynolds; *D* Corbis/John; *E* © Sue Lomas **p. 69** *B*, **p. 70** *E* © Sue Lomas. **p. 74** *A* John Conners Press Associates & PA Photos/Tim Ockenden. **p. 76** *A* Katz pictures. **p. 78** *A* Stock Market; *B* USGS **p. 79** *A, B* Stock Market. **pp. 80, 85, 97** *A, D, A* University of Dundee. **p. 82** *A* Corbis; *B, C* Stock market/Larry Williams. **p. 86** *A, D, G* University of Dundee IDENT **p. 95** *D* © John Hopkin. **p. 96** *F* Stock Market & Associated Press/Fredrik Funck & FLPA/Mark Newman & Corbis/Carl Purcell & Stock Market & James Davies Travel photography **p. 97** *C* Stock Market; *E* PA Photos/John Giles; *F* Media Skills. **p. 98** Corbis/John Noble. **p. 101** *C* Eye Ubiquitous. **p. 102** *D* Gettyone Stone. **p. 103** *E* Corbis/Wolfgang Kaehler. **p. 104** *A* & **p. 106** *A* Stock Market. **p. 109** *C, D* Panos Pictures. **p. 110** *B* Corbis/Morton Beebe, S.F.; *C* Still Pictures. **p. 111** *D* Gettyone Stone; *E* Stock Market. **p. 112** *A* Corbis/Charles & Josette Lenars; *B* Manila, Corbis/Paul A. Souders; *C* Corbis/Uwe Walz. **p. 113** *D* SPL/Rosenfled Images Ltd; *E* Gettyone Stone; *F* Panos Pictures; *G* Still Pictures/Martin Wyness. **p. 116** *B* Scotland in Focus/R Weir; *D* Scottish Viewpoint. **p. 118** *F* Corbis/Adam Woolfit. **p. 118** *G* StockScotland. **p. 119** *J* & **p. 120** *K* Scottish Viewpoint. **p. 123** *A* Sue Cunningham/SCP. **p. 124** *C* Corbis; *D* Sue Cunningham/SCP. **p. 125** *E* & **p. 126** *F* ©Sue Cunningham; *G* Environmental Images. **p. 128** *A* Press Association. **p. 129** *B* Newsteam International. **p. 132** *A* Scottish Viewpoint. **p. 133** *B* Still Pictures/Mike Jackson. **p. 136** *A* Coventry Evening Standard. **pp. 139** *A, B* Associated Press/Karel Prinsloo/Juda Ngwenya, Stringer. **p. 140** *C, D* Press Association. **p. 142** *A* Corbis; *B* George Bernard/Science Photo Library; *C* FLPA/Derek Hall; *D* PA Photos/EPA; *E* Oxford Scientific Films/Steve Turner. **p. 144** *A* Sue Cunningham; *A* FLPA/Silvestria **p. 146** *B* Oxford Scientific Films/Michael and Patricia Fogden. **p. 147** *D* Rex Features/SIPA. **p. 149** *E* Oxford Scientific Films/Tim Jackson; *F* Garden Matters; *G, H* LPA/W Wisniewski. **p. 152** *A* Scottish Viewpoint, *B* FLPA/S Jonasson, *C* Corbis; *D* FLPA/Martin Smith. **p. 153** *E* Eye Ubiquitous/Lawson Wood; *F* Oxford Scientific Films/Doug Allan. **p. 157** *D* Eye Ubiquitous/Damian Peters; *E, F* Dover, Tasmania. **p. 160** *A* Oxford Scientific Films/Scott Winer; *B* FLPA/Silvestria. **p. 161** *D* FLPA/Minden Pictures.

Text, Maps and Diagrams
p. 4 Philip Duffy; **pp. 13, 55, 117, 116, 119, 120, 118, 60, 54, 135** Maps reproduced from Ordnance Survey mapping with the permission of the Controller of Her Majesty's Stationery Office, © Crown copyright. All rights reserved. Licence no. 100000230; **p. 140** Guardian News Service Ltd. **p. 37** 'After the Earthquake' by Angela Topping, from CAN YOU HEAR? © Angela Topping. **p. 41** *M* © EERI report. **p. 47** *D*, *E* SITREP 16/ 13 March 2000, UNICEF. **p. 73** www.bbc.co.uk **p. 137** Environment Agency report. Used with permission. **p. 139** The effects of Mozambique': Chris McGreal, © The Guardian, 10 March 2000. *A, B* Chris McGreal by Chris McGreal, The Guardian, 4 March 2000. 'p. 140 © Daily Telegraph, 29 March, 2000. **p. 148** © www.guardianunlimited.co.uk. All used with permission.

Picture Research by: Debra Weatherly

Cover Photo by: Alamy

Throughout the book these symbols are used with activities that use literacy, numeracy and ICT skills.

Contents

Websites On pages where you are asked to go to www.heinemann.co.uk/hotlinks to complete a task or download information, please insert the code **5430P** at the website.

Making connections

Learn about

In this unit you will learn about the connections between places in different parts of the world and how they are connected to places you know.

You will also find out how to carry out an enquiry. This is the way that geographers find out more about things they want to know. You will learn:

- how to locate places on atlas maps
- how to ask geographical questions
- how to collect and present data
- how to make conclusions.

A An oasis in the Sahara desert, near Timbuktu, Mali

B The River Amazon, Brazil

C Bombay, India

D Glasgow, Scotland

F St Lucia

E The North Pole

G Sydney, Australia

H Mount Fuji, Japan

Activities

1 Choose one of the photographs **A**–**H**. Think of some questions you would like to ask to find out more about the place it shows. Write your questions down.

2 Choose the four questions that you think are most important. Then prepare an *annotated* sketch of the area in your photograph like the one in **I**, answering all the questions you have asked. If needed, use an atlas, books from the library, CD-ROMS or the Internet to gather your information. (ICT)

... draw an annotated sketch

A sketch that is *annotated* has labels describing its main features. Sometimes these labels will explain a feature too.

Animals are adapted to the hot, dry **climate**, like the camel which has a hump to store water.

People's clothes are light in colour to reflect the heat and to keep them cool.

The sky is blue with very little cloud, so the weather is very hot during the day.

There is little rainfall in this area so most of the ground is bare.

This is a natural environment.

Trees grow where there is a water supply, for example at an oasis.

I An annotated sketch of an oasis

Activities

3 Look at photographs **A**–**H**. Put the photos into pairs by making connections between them. For example, **A** and **B** both show trees as the main type of vegetation. There is more than one correct answer – your answer is right as long as you have found a good connection.

4 Copy the table below. Write down the letters for each of your pairs with a short explanation of the connection. The first one has been done for you.

Pair	Connection
A and B	Both show trees as the main vegetation

Where in the world?

All the places in the photographs on pages 4 and 5 can be found using an *atlas*. An atlas is a book of maps which shows different physical and human features of the world.

The *contents page* of an atlas is found at the front. It contains lists of different countries or continents. It also lists maps which show other things about a country or continent, like types of farming or different climate areas – these are known as *thematic* maps. You can see a typical contents page in **A**.

The *index* at the back of the atlas will help you find a particular place. Places are listed in alphabetical order. The entry will give the page number and a grid square reference, and the latitude and longitude may also appear. The index entry for Glasgow is shown in **B**, and map **D** shows an extract from an atlas that includes Glasgow.

A

BRITISH ISLES SECTION

2–3	**British Isles from Space**
4–5	**England and Wales**
6	**Scotland**
7	**Ireland**
8	**British Isles:** Relief
9	**British Isles:** Counties and Regions

Glasgow	**6**	**D4**	55 °N	4 °W
place or feature	*page*	*grid square*	*latitude*	*longitude*

B

Activities

1. Find each of the following features on map **D** opposite.

   a Glasgow
   b Stirling
   c Dumfries
   d Firth of Clyde
   e Loch Katrine
   f Arran.

2. Copy the table below. Complete it for features **a–f** above. The first one has been done for you.

Feature	Grid square	Description
Glasgow	D4	City

3. a Write the name of the place you live in as an atlas entry.

   b Choose two or more places that you know in other countries. Write out their atlas entries.

4. Use the satellite image **C** to find the places in question **1**.

C Satellite image of western Scotland

help!

C is a true-colour photo of part of the area shown in **D**. The brown areas are hills; the pinkish-grey areas show **settlements** and the green and yellow areas show **vegetation**.

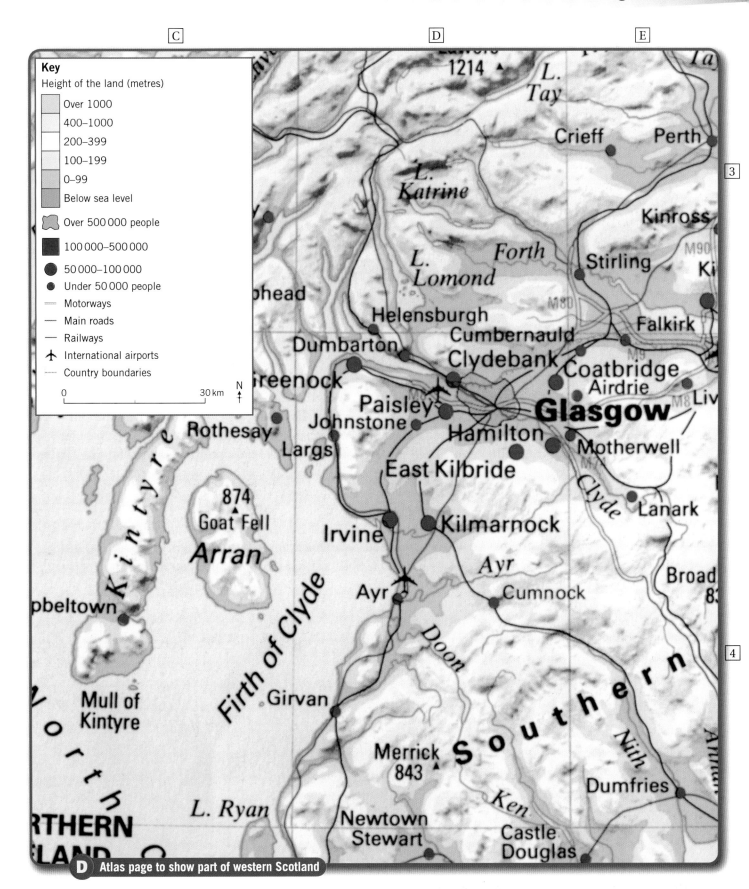

C   D   E

Key

Height of the land (metres)

- Over 1000
- 400–1000
- 200–399
- 100–199
- 0–99
- Below sea level
- Over 500 000 people
- 100 000–500 000
- 50 000–100 000
- Under 50 000 people
- Motorways
- Main roads
- Railways
- ✈ International airports
- Country boundaries

0   30 km   N

3

4

1214 ▲

L. Tay

Crieff   Perth

L. Katrine

Kinross

Forth

Stirling   Ki

L. Lomond

M90

M80

Helensburgh

Falkirk

...head

Cumbernauld

...reenock

Dumbarton

Clydebank

Coatbridge

M9

Airdrie

Liv

Rothesay

Paisley

Glasgow

M8

Johnstone

Hamilton

Motherwell

Largs

East Kilbride

874 ▲
Goat Fell

Clyde

Lanark

Arran

Kilmarnock

Irvine

Ayr

...pbeltown

Broad
83...

Firth of Clyde

Ayr

Cumnock

Mull of
Kintyre

Doon

Southern

Girvan

Nith

Merrick
843 ▲

Dumfries

L. Ryan

Ken

RTHERN

Newtown
Stewart

Castle
Douglas

...LAND

D   Atlas page to show part of western Scotland

Where are we?

Figure **A** is a photograph of the world taken from a satellite. Actually, it is made up of lots of photographs taken at different times as the satellite circled the Earth, because you cannot see the whole surface of the Earth at the same time. This is because the Earth is a sphere. It is also impossible to draw an accurate map of the world on a flat surface. In the drawing of the globe below only half the world can be seen. To represent the whole Earth as in the photograph, some places will be squashed up and some stretched.

Lines of latitude are imaginary lines drawn around the Earth from east to west. The line of latitude around the centre of the Earth is called the **Equator**. Latitude is measured in degrees north (N) or south (S) of the Equator.

Lines running north to south around the Earth pass through the North and South Poles and are called **lines of longitude**. They are all the same length. The line 0° of longitude passes through Greenwich, near London, and is called the Prime Meridian. Lines of longitude are numbered in degrees east (E) and west (W) of the Prime Meridian (see **B**).

So that places can be found exactly, each degree of latitude and longitude is divided into 60 **minutes**. Every place has a latitude and longitude co-ordinate, for example Glasgow is at 55°N 4°W.

Activity

1. Copy out the table below. It shows the latitude and longitude of some places, including those in the photographs on pages 4 and 5. Use an atlas to complete the table.

Place	Latitude	Longitude	Place	Latitude	Longitude
Timbuktu	16°N		North Pole	90°N	0°E
Glasgow		4°W	St Lucia	14°N	
River Amazon		50°W	Venice		12°E
Bombay	18°N		Sydney		
Mount Fuji	35°N		Salt Lake City		

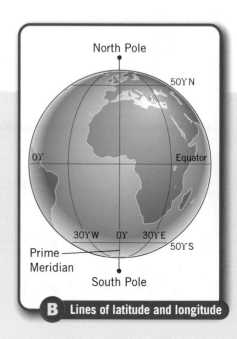

Passport to the world

There are lots of places around the world that we have links to every day. This is a picture of Jenny sitting at home in her kitchen. The picture is labelled with some of the places she has had contacts with today.

A

She is watching *Neighbours*, which is made in Australia.

Jenny's CD player was made in Japan.

Jenny's top was made in China.

Jenny has had a letter from her French penfriend today.

Her trainers were made in Thailand.

The floor covering was made in Wales.

Jenny's jeans are Levis. They were made in the USA.

She has eaten an Indian meal for her tea. The rice came from the Ganges valley.

Activities

❶ Make a list of all the places and countries which Jenny has had links with today. Mark them onto a world map. Use an atlas to help you.

❷ Give your map a key and a title to include the words *linked*, *places*, *world*.

❸ Make your own list of places in a world diary. Keep this diary for a month and then show all the places you have been linked to on a world map. Keep this list and the work you do with it in your World Passport.

Enquire within

The questions that geographers ask about people and places can often be answered by what they call an **enquiry** or investigation. When you carry out an enquiry there are a series of steps to follow. In the next pages you are going to learn about these steps and carry out an enquiry of your own.

Step 1: Asking questions

Geographers often carry out an enquiry to find out about a problem or issue in their local area. Sometimes they want to test a **hypothesis** (theory) or idea that they have about something. An enquiry may also be carried out to help people make a decision about something. For example, a company may have applied for planning permission to open a new fast food restaurant in your area. An enquiry question that you might like to ask is:

Why are fast food restaurants located where they are?

What sort of information do you need to help you make a decision about this?

Some questions you might like to ask include:

- What is fast food and what are fast food restaurants like?
- Who uses fast food restaurants and where do they come from?
- Is there a need for more fast food restaurants in the area?
- What effects do fast food restaurants have on the area around them?
- What alternatives are there to providing another restaurant?

How to ...

... ask geographical questions

Nearly all geographical questions will include at least one of the words:
- what?
- how?
- where?
- who?
- why?

If there are many things you want to ask about, you should ask several short questions.

A Inside a fast food restaurant

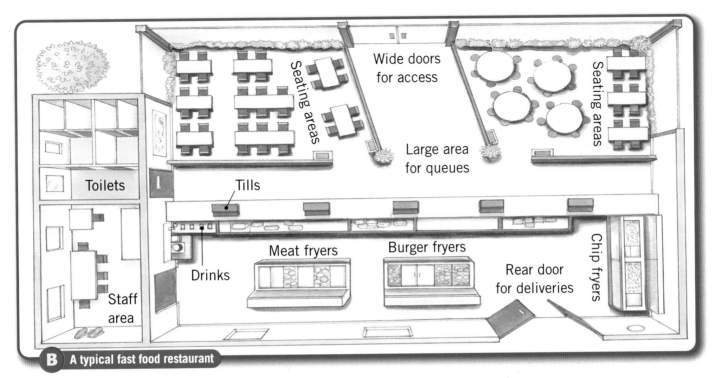

B A typical fast food restaurant

What are the features of a fast food restaurant?

The sketch in **B** above shows a typical fast food restaurant. There are several features that are common to fast food restaurants but which are not typical of other types of restaurants.

Activities

1 Copy the following table, which shows features of a fast food restaurant. Give reasons to explain why restaurants have these features. The first one has been done for you. Then add some features of your own, and explanations for them.

Description	Explanation
Food is designed to be eaten without cutlery	Saves washing up, so fewer people need to be employed
Self-service	
Open-plan restaurants	
Several serving points	
Large signs on the outside of the restaurant	
A lot of disposable wrapping material	

2 Use the ideas you have collected to make a poster advertising a fast food restaurant, pointing out the features you have mentioned in your table. Your poster should try to persuade a group of people to come and eat at your restaurant. Choose from:

ⓖ school friends

ⓖ parents with young children

ⓖ single people who live alone.

You could use the desktop publishing software on your computer.

Step 2: Gathering information

Once you have decided which questions to ask, you must decide how you are going to find the answers to them. Some questions are easy to answer straight away. For others you need to find out more detailed information, from books, from visiting places or from asking other people questions. The information geographers can gather can be divided into two types:

- **Primary data** is information that you find out for yourself by looking, counting or asking people questions.

- **Secondary data** is information that you gather by looking at maps or books, or by using CD-ROMS or the Internet.

Gathering primary data using a questionnaire

Suppose that you want to find out about the types of fast food restaurants that your class likes to visit. You might choose to use a questionnaire, or you might want to make a survey of what types of restaurant are available in your town. You could investigate how far it is to the restaurants from each person's home, or which type of fast food your class likes best.

How to …

… use a questionnaire

- Decide on the things you want to find out about.
- Try to ask questions which have answers that can be put into categories.
- Give some choices for people to give as an answer.
- Don't ask too many questions – people get bored!
- You could use a data-handling program to help you. **ICT**

Activity

1. Some students have designed questionnaire **C** about fast food.
   Look at each question carefully and give a reason why the students wanted to ask it.

> **1** **Which age group do you belong to?**
>
> 0–15 ☐   16–25 ☐   26–40 ☐
>
> 41–60 ☐   over 60 ☐
>
> **2** **Where do you live?**   In a town/city centre ☐
>
> In the suburbs ☐   In the countryside ☐
>
> **3** **Do you like fast food?**   Yes ☐   No ☐
>
> **4** **If yes, what is your favourite fast food?**
>
> Burgers ☐
>
> Pizza ☐
>
> Chicken ☐
>
> Fish'n'chips ☐
>
> Other ☐   Please name _____
>
> **5** **How far away from your home is your nearest fast food restaurant?**
>
> Under 1 km ☐   1–3 km ☐   3–6 km ☐   more than 6 km ☐

C

Gathering secondary data using maps

Another way to gather information is by using maps. You could, for example, use a map to find out what types of fast food restaurants are available in your town or city. Map **D** shows the layout of part of a city centre.

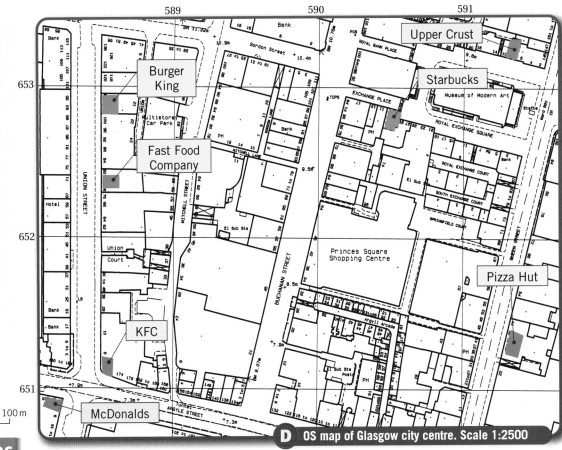

D OS map of Glasgow city centre. Scale 1:2500

Scale
0   100 m

Activities

1. On a copy of map **D**, colour in all the fast food restaurants.

2. Imagine you have to visit all the restaurants to make a survey of their features. Work out a route that allows you to visit all of them. Draw your route onto your map.

3. Use the scale to work out how far you will have to walk. The instructions in the How to … box will help you. ①②③

4. Write a description of your route to tell someone else how to follow it.

5. What do you notice about the location of the restaurants?

How to ...

... measure distances on a map

Measure the distance you have to travel by following these instructions.

1. Take a piece of paper with a straight edge.

2. Place the straight edge between the beginning and end of your journey.

3. Mark the two points on your piece of paper.

4. Move the paper to the scale line at the edge of the map.

5. With the first point on 0, read the distance you would have to travel on the scale line.

E Measuring distances on a map

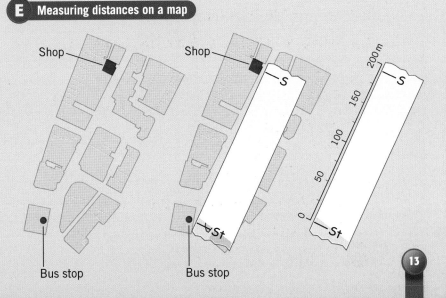

Step 3: Processing your information

Once you have gathered your data, you need to process or change it from simple written answers and numbers into graphs, maps or diagrams. These should show the information in a more interesting way and make it easier to understand.

Investigating McDonald's in Great Britain

The first McDonald's restaurant opened in the USA in 1955. McDonald's opened its first UK restaurant in London in 1974. The restaurant was very popular and the company opened more and more restaurants in the London area. Then, with an increase in demand between 1980 and 1988, the restaurants spread northwards through the main cities of England, Wales and eventually Scotland. Today there are over 860 restaurants throughout Great Britain. Table **G** below shows how the restaurants have spread.

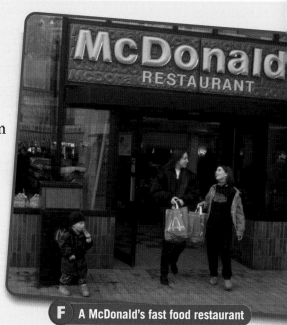

F A McDonald's fast food restaurant

Year	London	South-east England	Midlands	East Anglia	North-west England	North-east England	South-west England	Wales	Scotland	Total
1980	47	2	0	2	0	0	0	0	0	51
1988	106	32	46	20	46	24	2	10	8	294
1998	194	120	122	61	124	73	65	32	45	836

G McDonald's restaurants in Great Britain

1980

Key
restaurants
- 0
- 1–50
- 51–100
- 100+

0   300 km

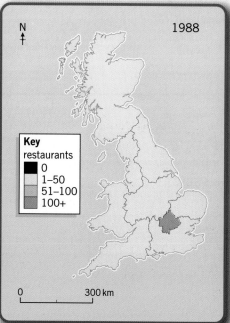

1988

Key
restaurants
- 0
- 1–50
- 51–100
- 100+

0   300 km

1998

Key
restaurants
- 0
- 1–50
- 51–100
- 100+

0   300 km

H This set of maps shows the growth of McDonald's restaurants in Great Britain since 1980

Activities

1. Use the writing frame to describe the growth of McDonald's in Great Britain. 📖

2. Use blank copies of a map showing the regions of Great Britain. Draw graphs to show the distribution of restaurants, using the data from table **G**. (123)

   a. Using the data for 1980, make a bar chart of the information, with a bar located in each region.

   b. Using the data for 1988, make a pictogram map of the information. What symbol could you use to show the information?

   c. Using the data for 1998, make a dot map of the information, following the instructions below.

3. Compare the maps and graphs you have drawn.

   a. Which was the quickest to draw?

   b. Which map or graph shows the information in the best way? Give reasons for your answer.

   c. Can you think of any other ways you could have shown the information?

4. Compare your maps to map **I** of population distribution in Great Britain. Are there any similarities and differences between the maps?

Growth of McDonald's in Great Britain

In 1974 McDonald's opened its first restaurant in Great Britain.

By 1980 there were restaurants in _____

By 1988 there were restaurants in _____

In 1998 the number of restaurants had grown to _____ and they could be found _____

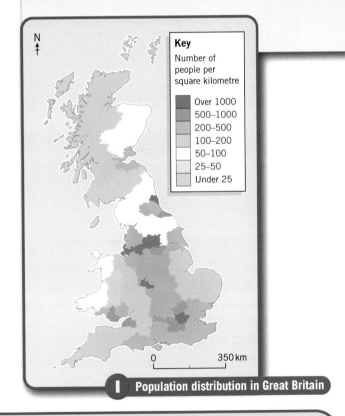

Key
Number of people per square kilometre

- Over 1000
- 500–1000
- 200–500
- 100–200
- 50–100
- 25–50
- Under 25

0   350 km

I | **Population distribution in Great Britain**

How to...

... draw a dot distribution map

1. You are going to show the distribution of McDonald's restaurants in 1998 on a map of Great Britain by drawing dots in each region.

2. Find the number of restaurants in the region from table **G**.

3. Use one dot for every ten restaurants:
   - ◎ Divide the number of restaurants by 10.
   - ◎ Give the number to the nearest 10; for London, 194/10 = 19.4 = 19 dots.

4. Draw the dots evenly over the region on your map.

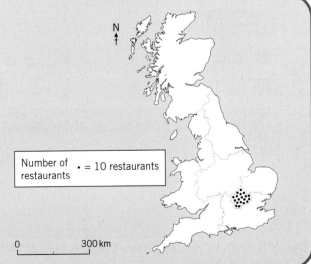

Number of restaurants   • = 10 restaurants

0   300 km

Investigating McDonald's around the world

McDonald's is a **transnational** company. This means that it does business all over the world. In 2000, McDonald's had more than 26 000 restaurants worldwide in 119 countries on five continents. This means that every minute of the day someone is eating a McDonald's for their lunch!

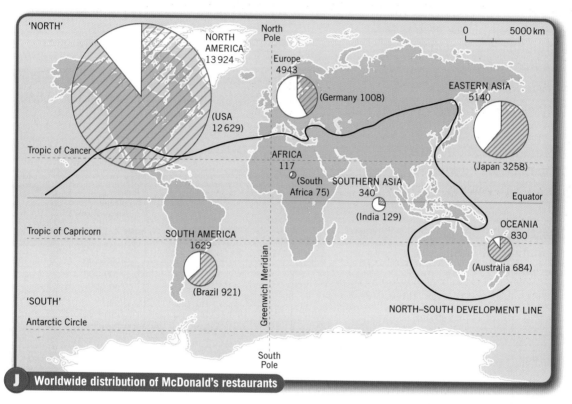

J | Worldwide distribution of McDonald's restaurants

Map **J** shows some of the countries where McDonald's have restaurants. It also shows the total number of restaurants for each continent. The world has been divided into two by the North–South Development Line. This is an imaginary line that separates More Economically Developed Countries (the richer countries, mainly in North America, Europe and Oceania) from the Less Economically Developed Countries. These are the poorer countries, mainly in South America, Asia and Africa.

Activities

1. Study the map. Do you notice any difference between 'North' and 'South'?

2. Use the writing frame to describe the distribution of the restaurants.

> ### Worldwide distribution of McDonald's restaurants
>
> McDonald's have restaurants in the continents of _____
>
> They have very few restaurants in _____
>
> This is because_____
>
> On the other hand, they have many restaurants in _____
>
> This is because _____

Step 4: Drawing conclusions

By this stage in your enquiry you have gathered all the information you need to answer your question. You have displayed the results as a series of graphs, maps and diagrams, explaining what these show. You must now come to some conclusions about them.

A conclusion:

- looks at all the work you have done
- links the results to the questions you asked at the beginning
- evaluates the strengths and weaknesses of the work as a whole
- makes suggestions about further investigations you might carry out.

Our main enquiry question was:

Why are fast food restaurants located where they are?

In your conclusion you should:

> *Give the features of a fast food restaurant.*
> *Say which you think are the most important.*

> *Describe the distribution of fast food restaurants in a town centre.*

> *Summarise the results of your questionnaire, saying what people think about fast food restaurants.*

> *Describe and give reasons for the distribution of McDonald's restaurants around the world.*

You may want to start your conclusion something like this:

> From our study of fast food restaurants it is clear that they have many features which make them different from other types of café or restaurant. The most important features are the things which allow the food to be served quickly and conveniently. For example, the restaurants are self-service, they have many service tills ...

Presenting your conclusions in different ways

A conclusion is not often the place where you present more graphs or maps. It is usually only writing. But sometimes it is possible to use a diagram or photograph which presents your information with more impact. The boxes show three ways of making your conclusions clearer.

A time line   1970   1980   1990   2000

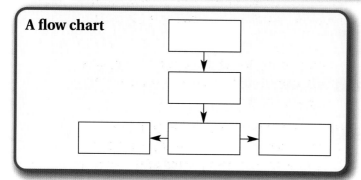

A flow chart

A **summary chart** could give reasons for the growth of fast food restaurants and indicate which are the most important **factors** in their location.

Evaluating your work

An **evaluation** of your work should finish off your enquiry.
It refers to the whole of the project and should look at the *strengths,* such as:

- what you found most interesting or useful in your work
- what you think went well.

It also looks at the *weaknesses*:

- the problems or difficulties you had collecting information
- if it would have been better to collect more or different information.

You can also suggest ideas for further investigations:

- Would a study of another fast food chain like Wimpy or Harry Ramsden's give you the same results?
- In what ways would the locations of Drive-thru restaurants be different?

Activity

Research activity

1 What do we know, think and feel about other places?

  a Choose a place mentioned in this unit that you would like to visit.

  b Find out all you can about it. Use all the resources you have used in this unit, such as atlases, newspapers, CD-ROMS, Internet and textbooks. **ICT**

  c Prepare a brochure for tourists telling them what the place is like. Illustrate it with pictures, maps and diagrams.

Review and reflect

Activities

1. You can now use all the things you have learned about in this unit to carry out an investigation about the place where you live. Follow the route to enquiry:

   1. **Asking questions** – How is our place connected to other places?

   2. **Gathering information** – make up a questionnaire to ask people you know about the connections they have with other places. You could ask where their parents were born, where they go on holiday, or where they shop. *Use the work you did on page 12 to help you with this.*

   3. **Processing your information** – use the results of your survey to make maps and diagrams to show what you have found out. Write a description of what they show. *Look back at the writing frames used to describe patterns on pages 15–16.*

   4. **Drawing conclusions** – look back at the original question and explain what you have found out about your place's connections to other places. Remember to say what part of your enquiry went well and what part could have been improved. *Some ideas for this were given on page 18.*

Things you have learned about	Pages	Examples
Using an atlas		Finding places in western Scotland
Measuring distances on maps		Finding how far to walk between restaurants in a city centre
Finding places using latitude and longitude	8–9	Giving the location of the pictures
Planning routes on maps		
Describing patterns on maps		
Drawing annotated sketches		
Carrying out an enquiry		

2. Make a large copy of the table. Fill in the things you have learned about or done for each of the parts of this unit. Examples have been given to help you.

3. Write down three important skills you have learnt from this unit and explain why you chose them.

4. Write down two things that you did or learned that might be useful later on in your geography studies, for example, measuring distances on maps.

5. Write down any activities you found difficult, and say why.

Earthquakes and volcanoes

Learn about

A volcanic eruption or an earthquake can be disastrous, especially if it is in a place where many people live. Understanding the causes and effects of volcanoes and earthquakes can help people to manage the problems that they cause. In this unit you will learn:

- what volcanoes and earthquakes are and where they occur

  - what happens when a volcano erupts
  - how volcanic eruptions affect different places in the world in different ways
  - what happens in an earthquake
  - how people can try to reduce the effects of earthquakes
  - how aid can help earthquake and volcano victims
  - why people want to live in active zones.

Activities

Discussion activity

1. Look carefully at the photographs on these two pages.

   a Which do you think are about **earthquakes** and which are about **volcanoes**? What are your reasons for thinking this?

   b For each photograph, agree on at least two things it tells you about earthquakes or volcanoes.

   c Do the photographs show the *causes* or the *effects* of earthquakes and volcanoes?

2. These are all dramatic or negative images about earthquakes and volcanoes. What positive effects do you think earthquakes and volcanoes can have on people and places?

3. Start to make a word bank of the key words and terms you have used – begin with *earthquake*, *volcano*, *cause* and *effect*.

Where do earthquakes and volcanoes occur?

In geography it is important to be able to recognise and describe patterns on the Earth's surface. Have a look at the map below, which shows more of the world's strongest earthquakes and active volcanoes. The patterns of earthquakes and volcanoes give us some clues about why they happen.

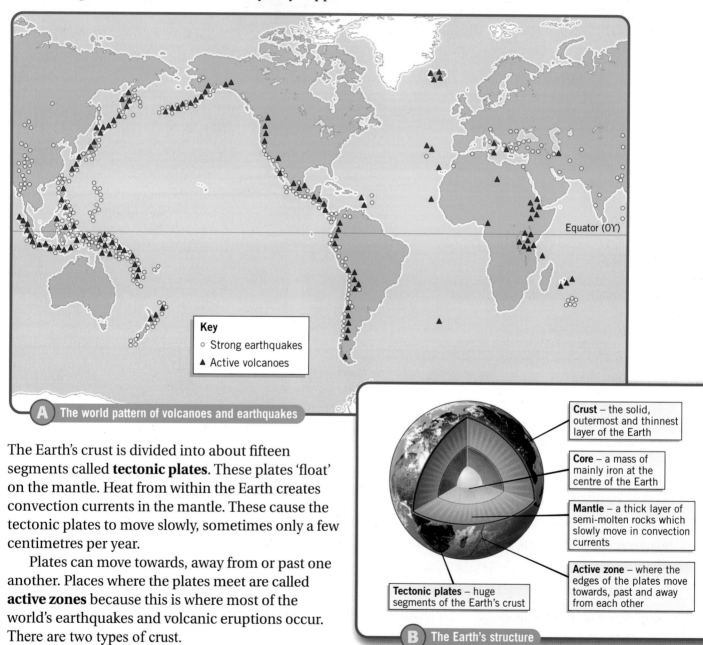

Key
○ Strong earthquakes
▲ Active volcanoes

Equator (0Y)

A The world pattern of volcanoes and earthquakes

The Earth's crust is divided into about fifteen segments called **tectonic plates**. These plates 'float' on the mantle. Heat from within the Earth creates convection currents in the mantle. These cause the tectonic plates to move slowly, sometimes only a few centimetres per year.

Plates can move towards, away from or past one another. Places where the plates meet are called **active zones** because this is where most of the world's earthquakes and volcanic eruptions occur. There are two types of crust.

Crust – the solid, outermost and thinnest layer of the Earth

Core – a mass of mainly iron at the centre of the Earth

Mantle – a thick layer of semi-molten rocks which slowly move in convection currents

Active zone – where the edges of the plates move towards, past and away from each other

Tectonic plates – huge segments of the Earth's crust

B The Earth's structure

- ⊚ *Continental crust* is lighter, thick (35–70 km) and very old (over 1500 million years).
- ⊚ *Oceanic crust* is heavier, thin (6–10 km) and young (mostly less than 200 million years).

Activities

1. Write a definition for the word *describe* in your word bank.

2. Make a list of words that would help you describe the distribution of volcanoes and earthquakes shown on map **A**.

3. Write a description of the world distribution of volcanoes and earthquakes using the words from your word list. Use the *How to ...* box to help you to write a good geographical description.

How to ...

... describe patterns on maps

- Begin with a **general statement**, e.g. *'The map shows that volcanoes and earthquakes are found ...'.*

- Go on to give greater **detail** about where in the world they are and are not found.

- Include **place names**, e.g. *countries, continents, seas, oceans, mountain ranges ...*

- Mention **directions** for the patterns: *... north to south, ... to the south-west*, etc.

Activities ICT

Investigating earthquakes on the internet

Map **C** was taken from the earthquake area of the National Earthquake Information Centre website. Answer these questions using the map and an atlas.

1. In which country was the most recent earthquake event?

2. What was the magnitude (strength) and depth of this earthquake?

3. What was the depth of the deepest recent earthquake? In which country did it happen?

4. What was the magnitude of the strongest earthquake? In which country did it happen?

Now download today's national earthquake map from the United States Geological Survey (go to www.heinemann.co.uk/hotlinks and enter code 543OP). Use this map to answer questions **1–4** above and as a record of your completed work.

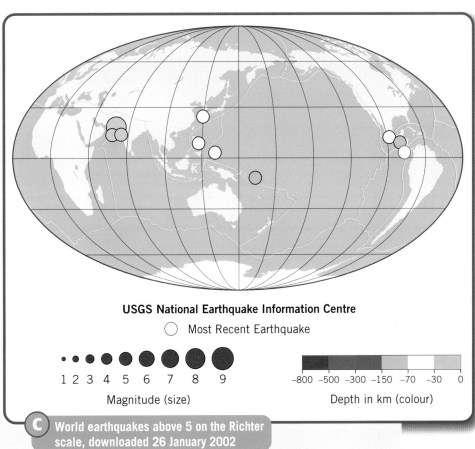

USGS National Earthquake Information Centre

○ Most Recent Earthquake

1 2 3 4 5 6 7 8 9
Magnitude (size)

−800 −500 −300 −150 −70 −30 0
Depth in km (colour)

C World earthquakes above 5 on the Richter scale, downloaded 26 January 2002

Why do volcanoes and earthquakes occur where they do?

The Earth has a thin **crust**. Scientists think that this crust is divided up into a number of different-sized sections, called tectonic plates, which move slowly in different directions. Some, like the North American and Eurasian Plates, are moving away from one another. Others, like the Nazca and South American Plates, are moving towards each other. Finally, in some parts of the world the plates are moving sideways past each other, as along the San Andreas Fault in the western USA. Earthquakes and volcanoes occur mainly in active zones at the edges of tectonic plates.

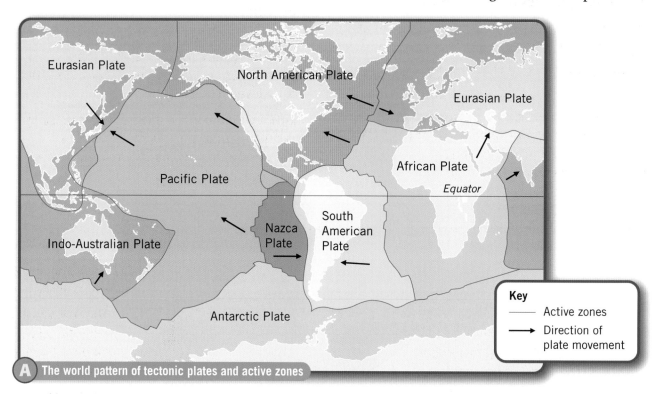

A The world pattern of tectonic plates and active zones

Activities

1. Make a copy of the table and complete it by looking at map **A** above. Decide in each case whether the plates are moving together or moving apart. The first one has been done for you.

Plates	Movement
Eurasian and North American	Moving apart
Nazca and South American	
Eurasian and Pacific	
South American and African	
African and Eurasion	

2. Look again at map **A** on page 22, map **A** above and your completed table. What do you notice about the link between the world pattern of volcanoes and earthquakes and the world pattern of tectonic plates?

What are volcanoes?

Volcanoes are openings (**vents**) in the Earth's crust where **magma** (molten rock) from inside the Earth is able to escape to the surface. The magma can appear in a number of different forms:

- as liquid **lava** (molten rock) that flows down the volcano sides
- as **volcanic bombs** – lumps of molten rock that solidify as they fall from the sky
- as hot ash and dust which are thrown into the air and eventually settle on the surrounding land
- as steam and gases, which may be poisonous.

Volcanic eruptions are strongly influenced by the type of magma that escapes. Some are very explosive and dangerous. When Mount Pinatubo in the Philippines erupted in 1991, it sent up a cloud of ash and steam 30 km high. About 700 people died as a result of the eruption.

Other eruptions are more gentle. Kilauea, one of the Hawaiian Islands, has been continuously pouring out runny lava since 1983 with little threat to humans.

Volcanoes may be active, dormant or extinct.

- **Active volcanoes** are those that have erupted within historical time and are likely to erupt again. There are over 700 active volcanoes in the world.
- **Dormant volcanoes** are currently inactive but may erupt again. Most of the Cascade volcanoes on the west coast of North America are believed to be dormant.
- **Extinct volcanoes** are those that are unlikely to erupt again in the future. There are a number of extinct volcanoes in Britain, such as the one Edinburgh Castle is built on.

A Volcanic eruption on the island of Heimaey, Iceland

Activities

1. Use photograph **A** to draw a 'wordscape'.

   First draw a simple outline sketch. Include outlines of the main features.

2. Next, choose nouns and adjectives that describe the different areas of the photograph.

3. Carefully write the words onto the outline sketch. Shape the words to fit the features in the photograph they describe.

A virtual field trip up Stromboli

A Stromboli – Station 14, Italy

B Aerial photo of Stromboli

Stromboli is one of the Aeolian Islands, a group of volcanic islands located between Sicily and the Italian mainland. It is one of the most active volcanoes on Earth. It has been in nearly continuous eruption for around 2000 years. The island is about 2 km in diameter. Its highest point is 924 metres above sea level but it rises over 3000 metres above the floor of the Tyrrhenian Sea.

In 1991 the population of the island was 361. However, during the summer months there are many more residents, mainly due to tourism.

C Location of Stromboli

Activities

Imagine that your class is going on a one-day geography field trip to study Stromboli, an active volcano. Carry out some research using the website: 'Stromboli Online' at www.heinemann.co uk/hotlinks; enter code 5430P and find the links for this page.

1 a Collect information using these headings:

- Population and settlement
- Transport
- Shops
- Weather and climate
- Vegetation
- Tourist information
- Health and safety (including possible hazards).

b When do you think is the best time of year to carry out the field trip?

c What else do you need to know in order to plan, and why?

2 Choose the items you should carry up the volcano in your rucksack. To carry it comfortably, your backpack should weigh no more than 7.5 kg. Table **D** lists the possible items to choose from and their weights. To help you make sensible choices, use your research from question 1.

3 Carry out a *virtual field trip* at 'Stromboli Online'.

a Before you begin, check out today's weather conditions using links from the website to both satellite images and weather stations (Napoli is the nearest).

b Choose whichever virtual route you prefer. As you ascend the volcano, collect the following information:

- the altitude at each station
- photographs
- at least one annotated field sketch
- changing vegetation types.

4 At the end of the field trip evaluate your rucksack contents. Which were the good and poor choices? Why?

Contents	Weight	Contents	Weight
2 litres bottled water	2 kg	Suntan lotion	200 g
Food for one day	1.5 kg	Sandals	200 g
Trainers	800 g	Clipboard	200 g
Binoculars	800 g	Spare T-shirt	200 g
Jumper	700 g	Hat	150 g
Fleece	600 g	Insect repellent	100 g
Roll mat	500 g	Swimsuit / trunks	100 g
First aid kit	500 g	Map	50 g
Rucksack	500 g	Pencils	50 g
Camera and film	500 g	Money bag	50 g
Flask of hot drink	400 g	Compass	50 g
Towel	300 g	Sunglasses	50 g
Waterproof	300 g	Change of socks	50 g
Thermals	300 g	Change of underwear	50 g
Trowel	300 g		
Shorts	250 g		

D Items that you might need on your trip

What happens when a volcano erupts?

The Philippine Islands are located in an active zone on the edges of the Eurasian and Philippine Plates. This active zone is part of the 'Pacific Ring of Fire' where there are many volcanoes and earthquakes. Mount Pinatubo is one of 22 active volcanoes in the Philippines and is located about 100 km north-west of the capital city, Manila. After being dormant for more than 600 years, Pinatubo awoke with a bang on 9 June 1991. It caused one of the largest eruptions of the twentieth century.

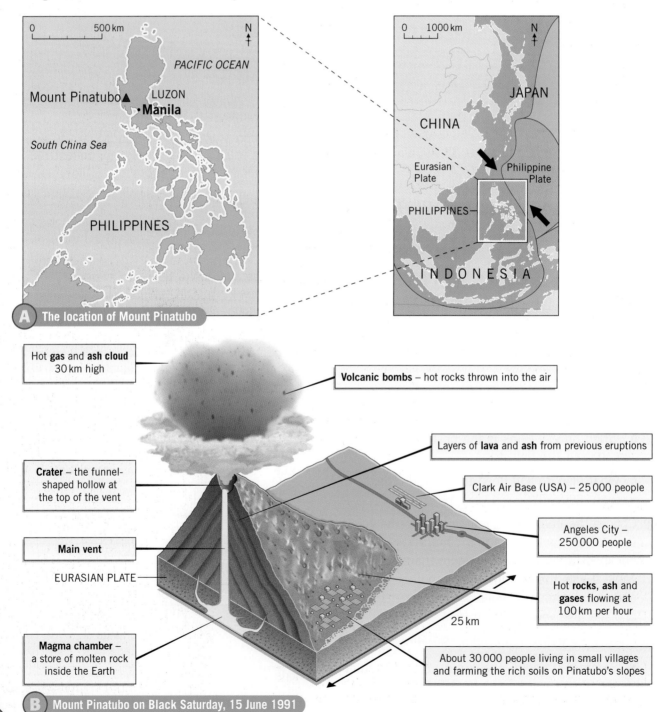

A The location of Mount Pinatubo

Hot **gas** and **ash cloud** 30 km high

Volcanic bombs – hot rocks thrown into the air

Crater – the funnel-shaped hollow at the top of the vent

Main vent

EURASIAN PLATE

Magma chamber – a store of molten rock inside the Earth

Layers of **lava** and **ash** from previous eruptions

Clark Air Base (USA) – 25 000 people

Angeles City – 250 000 people

Hot **rocks**, **ash** and **gases** flowing at 100 km per hour

25 km

About 30 000 people living in small villages and farming the rich soils on Pinatubo's slopes

B Mount Pinatubo on Black Saturday, 15 June 1991

The eruption of Mount Pinatubo

Extracts from the diary of Kimi Nath

C The eruption of Mount Pinatubo

When the Angeles City newspapers reported that a group of American volcano scientists had moved into the Clark Air Base, everyone was talking about Mount Pinatubo and saying, 'What volcano?' Many Filipinos had never heard of the volcano, which had been dormant for over 600 years.

Wednesday 12 June

Mount Pinatubo gave us the first taste of her fury. A deep, rumbling boom shook the earth, and an angry, dark cloud appeared in the distance. A cold wind blew around us. It was very eerie.

As the 'cloud' moved towards us, it spread out and the sun disappeared. Dust began to fall from the sky. By the time the 'cloud' drifted past us, 2 cm of ash coated the ground. The same thing happened on Thursday, and on Friday. Everyone was tense, wondering what would happen next. We didn't have to wait long before we found out.

D Ash on the cars at Clark Air Base

E Clark Air Base during the eruption

Saturday 15 June

The sun was shining brightly at 8.30 a.m. After clearing 5 to 6 cm of ash from my car, I drove to the Clark Air Base, just north of Angeles City, for a meeting. Around 9.00 a.m. a huge rumble shook the room, and the sky began to darken. By 9.30 it was midnight black. By a cruel twist of fate, a huge typhoon hit at the same time. Swirling winds mixed the heavy rain with ash so that mud fell from the sky. The force of the eruption was so strong that huge pieces of the volcano blew apart, so that rocks also rained down. Electricity, water and telephones all failed, so we sat in darkness. The muddy ash came down more heavily with each passing moment, and the 'rotten eggs' stench from the sulphur in the air made us sick. Sulphur fireballs shot blazing orange through the night, and the typhoon brought lightning, which exploded in fiery displays. Then the earthquakes began ... They came one after another, shifting the ground beneath us. Some were powerful enough to send things crashing to the ground and to crack the beams of the homes in which we huddled. With the awful storm outside and the earthquakes within, there was no safe place to go. Throughout 'Black Saturday' we huddled in fear and wondered if the world was truly coming to an end.

Sunday 16 June

We came out of our shelters cautiously and looked in awe on the grey devastation all around us. Our homes were buried in ash and hundreds of buildings had collapsed. Roads were blocked by mud, trees and vehicles; the power was still off and there wasn't much food or water. We knew things were never going to get back to normal ...

Pinatubo leaves behind a wasteland

Pinatubo's ash, dust and lahars (mudflows) have turned vast areas of farmland into a wasteland. The eruption has affected more than 249 000 families (1.2 million people), causing over 700 deaths and 184 injuries. Many more might have died, but fortunately warnings based on information from **seismographs** at the American Clark Air Base allowed the authorities to evacuate about 14 000 people from the area surrounding the volcano.

Water supplies, power lines, roads and bridges were badly damaged by the lahars. Houses and public buildings collapsed from the weight of ash. More than 650 000 workers are out of work because of the destruction of their farms, shops and factories.

The Americans were forced to evacuate Clark Air Base after volcanic dust, ash and lahars left its runways useless and endangered its planes. In Manila, 100 km away, the International Airport was also closed for four days and public buildings were turned into evacuation centres to house refugees from the devastated areas.

F Extract from *The Philippine Star*, 21 July 1991

G Mount Pinatubo's new crater lake, formed after the 1991 eruption

H Whole villages were covered in ash

Lahars swept away whole villages. Green rice paddies and sugar-cane fields were covered with ash. About 4000 square kilometres were affected, but people have since returned to farm the rich soils formed from the mud and ash.

I

Wildlife returns to Mount Pinatubo

Eight years after Pinatubo's hot gases stripped its trees of life and ash blanketed its slopes, wild cats, boars, deer and monkeys are returning to areas where plants have started to grow again. Snakes, such as boa

constrictors and cobras, and even monitor lizards are also appearing on the volcano's slopes.

Pinatubo's eruption threw 20 million tonnes of sulphur dioxide into the air. Scientists think that this caused a 1°C fall in global temperatures for over five years. The dust thrown into the atmosphere by Pinatubo may also add to global warming in the future.

J

K Extract from article by Ding Cervantes, 20 April 1999

This **satellite image** of the area around Mount Pinatubo was taken by the space shuttle Endeavour on 13 April 1994. The main **crater** and its lake can easily be seen in *blue*. The *pale pink* colour on the slopes of Pinatubo shows the ash deposited during the 1991 eruption. The *dark pink* areas show the lahars. These are still a hazard to the people who have returned to farm the area around the volcano. Every time rain falls on Mount Pinatubo, mud slides down from the highlands *(dark green)* on to villages, homes and fields. On the western side of the image the lahars spill into the South China Sea *(black)*. Satellite images can be very helpful in monitoring hazards such as lahars. This can stop lives being lost.

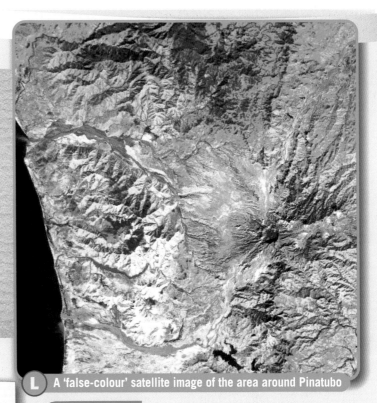

L A 'false-colour' satellite image of the area around Pinatubo

Angeles City
– well on the road to recovery

n 1990 Angeles City, 25 km to the east of Pinatubo, had a population of 250 000. Many of its industries supported the American Clark Air Base, just outside the city. When the 25 000 people living at the Air Base left after the eruption, farmers, furniture-makers, tailors, restaurants, auto-repair shops, hotels and night clubs, taxi-drivers, etc. were left without customers. Over 250 000 people lost their jobs as a result of the eruption of Pinatubo.

M Angeles City

After 1991, Angeles City began to grow as a tourist destination. It now has 24 restaurants, six new hotels, 30 night clubs, four Internet cafés and hundreds of small boutiques, pharmacies, photo shops and taxi companies, employing thousands of Filipinos. The tourist industry is now the biggest employer in the area. The government is spending large sums of money on attracting foreign visitors.

Activity

1 You have been asked by the Angeles City Tourist Information Office to produce a brochure for visitors to the region to inform them about the eruption of Mount Pinatubo in 1991. The brochure must include:

- an annotated cross-section showing what happened when Mount Pinatubo erupted

- an annotated map of the Pinatubo region locating features of the eruption

- written information about the area before, during and after the eruption

- a glossary of terms to help tourists understand exactly what happened and why

- illustrations that capture tourists' interest in the volcano – guides in Angeles City earn 300 Pesos (about £5) for each tour party they take up Mount Pinatubo.

help!

When you write your brochure, remember that good geographers:

- include specific facts, figures and place names in their work
- write information in their own words
- evaluate their work when it is finished.

What are earthquakes? Are they all identical?

Case Study

All the case study information on this page and the next is from the *BBC Online* website. It is a small selection of their news reports following the devastating Gujarat earthquake which struck India in January 2001.

Fact file: Gujarat, January 2001

- ⊚ **Time and date:** 8.46 am local time on 26 January 2001.
- ⊚ **Strength:** 7.9 on the Richter scale – India's biggest earthquake since 1956. Tremors were felt as far away as Bangladesh.
- ⊚ **Epicentre:** Near the town of Bhuj in Gujarat state, north-west India.
- ⊚ **Level of Economic Development:** India is an **LEDC**.

Quake epicentre near Bhuj

A Area affected by the Gujarat earthquake, 2001

What happened during the earthquake?

Dear Viki

I was just getting up and suddenly felt that a large group of monkeys were running around in the terrace because the room was shaking. The shakings didn't stop and became more severe. It was then that I suspected something big on the lines of an earthquake, but I couldn't believe it because Ahmadabad had never been hit by one.

I cannot describe the shaking to you. Just imagine how you would feel if someone very powerful took hold of your house and started shaking it right from the foundations. After about a minute it stopped. I have been lucky, by God's grace.

Vivek

B An e-mail from Vivek Iyer, an Ahmadabad doctor

The effects on buildings and infrastructure

Many lives could have been saved in the Gujarat earthquake if building codes had been enforced and cheap protection measures carried out, Indian scientists say.

One civil engineer from Bombay said: 'We are beginning to learn that governments are not prepared. They directly or indirectly contribute to the deaths by permitting poor construction quality.'

India, along with other developing countries, is undergoing rapid urbanisation, so buildings are being put up quickly to meet growing housing needs. Some developers, keen to make a quick profit, are not as concerned about safety as they should be.

C

• The effects on the people •

At least 30 000 people are estimated to have died in the quake. Another 55 000 have been injured and about half a million made homeless.

The authorities have turned their attention to long-term help for survivors, including setting up tent cities to shelter those made homeless by the quake.

As hopes of finding survivors fade, aid agencies are now trying to provide food, shelter and water to the families without homes.

Efforts are focusing on the need to cremate the thousands of dead to prevent the spread of disease. Many hospitals are treating people in the open air, and doctors say they are running out of bandages and medical supplies.

D News report, 30 January 2001

F Earthquake fault, Gujarat

E A young earthquake victim

Short-term responses to the earthquake

Aid from around the world has been pouring into India's earthquake zone. In a rare act, a plane from India's long-time rival Pakistan arrived carrying 2500 blankets and 200 tents for the quake survivors.

The United Nations Children's Fund has committed at least US $8 million in immediate aid. They have delivered thousands of blankets, a million chlorine tablets for purifying water, and plastic sheeting for shelter.

The UK, which has a large Indian community, has donated £10 million. It has also sent a team of 69 rescue workers on a military plane. Russia has sent a 59-strong team of medical and rescue experts, including doctors, a field hospital, and three dog teams.

G News report, 1 February 2001

The effects on the economy

The cost of India's quake

Gujarat is India's second largest industrial region, with many steel and textile mills. It has India's busiest port, Kandla. This earthquake will have an impact way beyond its state borders. Repairing buildings and installations is expected to cost around 150 billion rupees (£2.2 billion). It is an expense that India can ill afford. The government has asked the World Bank for a £1.1 billion loan to aid the rebuilding.

Industries hit

The diamond, pharmaceutical and textile industries are likely to be worst hit by the massive disruption to power lines, transport and telecommunications.

India's businesses are generally underinsured, so that more of the costs will be carried by local firms and individuals. Jobs will be lost and overall industrial production will fall. But steel and cement industries are likely to benefit from rebuilding the earthquake-hit region.

H News report, 2 February 2001

2 Present your earthquake case study under the following headings:
- What happened
- Effects on buildings and infrastructure
- Short- and long-term responses
- Effects on the economy
- Effects on the people

3 Add the geographical terms you have used to your word bank.

4 Compare your earthquake case study with those of others in your class.

Activities

You can find the *BBC Online* website at www.heinemann.co.uk/hotlinks
Enter code 5430P and follow the links to *one* recent earthquake to produce a **case study** like this one. ICT

1 Produce a fact file like the one on page 32 to introduce your earthquake case study.

What happens in an earthquake?

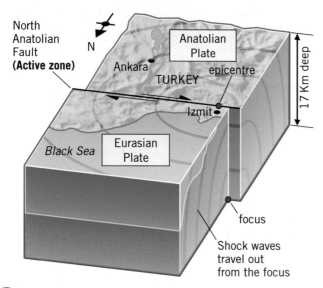

A The Izmit earthquake in Turkey, 17 August 1999

As we found out on page 22, the Earth is made up of three main layers – the **crust**, the **mantle** and the **core**. The crust is much thinner than the other layers and is the only layer of the Earth that humans have actually seen. The crust is broken up into tectonic plates which 'float' on the mantle. They are pushed slowly in different directions by the molten rock beneath. Active zones are created where tectonic plates move past one another.

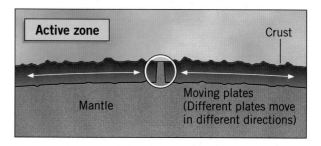

Earthquakes and volcanoes tend to occur in these zones.

Earthquakes are caused when two plates moving past one another become 'stuck' for a while so that tension builds up. Eventually the stress becomes so great that the crust breaks and moves suddenly. The point where the rock actually breaks is called the **focus**. This is usually found far beneath the surface of the Earth. The point on the surface directly above the focus is called the **epicentre**. When the plates move suddenly, **shock waves** are sent out in all directions. These waves can cause a lot of damage on the Earth's surface.

The magnitude or strength of an earthquake is measured using an instrument called a seismograph, which records the shaking of the ground. Look at the seismogram **B** for the Turkish earthquake in 1999. The magnitude is shown by the lines that go up and down. The stronger the quake, the longer will be the lines drawn on the graph. The length of time that a quake lasts is shown by the horizontal distance across the graph. The magnitude of an earthquake can be measured using the Richter scale (see **C**).

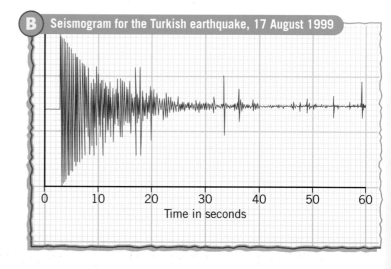

B Seismogram for the Turkish earthquake, 17 August 1999

Each point on the scale is actually ten times bigger than the one below it. This means that an earthquake measuring 6 on the Richter scale is ten times stronger than one measuring 5. Earthquakes below 2.5 are not usually felt by humans.

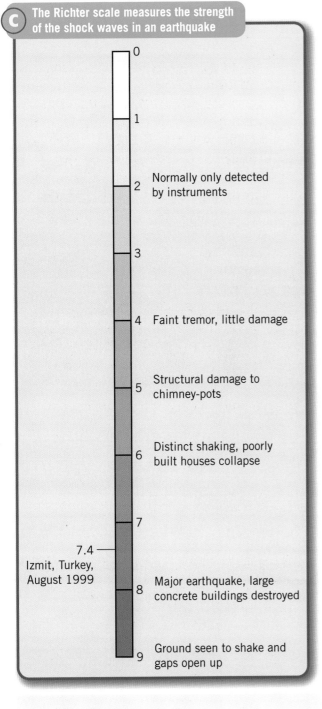

C The Richter scale measures the strength of the shock waves in an earthquake

0

1

2 Normally only detected by instruments

3

4 Faint tremor, little damage

5 Structural damage to chimney-pots

6 Distinct shaking, poorly built houses collapse

7

7.4 —
Izmit, Turkey,
August 1999

8 Major earthquake, large concrete buildings destroyed

9 Ground seen to shake and gaps open up

Activities

1 Copy out the passage below. Fill in the missing words to explain why the Izmit earthquake in Turkey in 1999 happened.

A huge earthquake measuring _____ on the Richter scale happened in Turkey on 17 August 1999. It was caused when two plates, the _____ Plate and the _____ Plate, became 'stuck' for a while. This caused stress to build up until the Earth's crust eventually broke, sending out _____ in all directions. The focus of the earthquake was about _____ below the Earth's surface. The earthquake lasted for about _____ seconds and was most violent during the first _____ seconds. Earthquakes and volcanoes often happen in active zones such as the _____ Fault.

Research activities

2 Find the name of a scale, other than the Richter scale, which is used to measure earthquakes.

3 Download a map from the Internet showing the most recent earthquakes in the world. At www.heinemann.co.uk/hotlinks enter code 5430P and follow the links for this page. (ICT)

a Draw a table like the one below. Fill in the details for each earthquake.

Country	Date	Magnitude	Depth

b Give the table a suitable title.

c How many of the earthquakes in your table have reached the national news?

d Why do you think this is the case?

How do earthquakes affect people and places?

Activities

Look at the photographs on this page and on pages 20 and 21. They suggest some of the ways in which earthquakes affect people's lives and the places they live. Use them to help you answer these questions. Try to add your own ideas as well.

1 Write down five sentences that describe how earthquakes affect people's lives and how people feel after an earthquake.

2 Now write down five sentences that describe how earthquakes affect places – buildings, transport links, services such as hospitals, electricity supplies, etc.

3 Compare your lists with those of another person. Add at least three of their ideas to your own.

4 Next, rank your list for question 1 according to how severely an earthquake would affect *your* family. Write down the effect that would have the most impact first.

5 Now rank your list for question 2 in the same way.

6 Look at the top two effects in each list. Explain why you decided that these would have the greatest impact.

After the Earthquake

Whether to cry out in answer to
My father's strangled cries
As he shifts bricks above my head,
Or whether to keep silent, holding back
This dust with clamped lips. I lie   5
Sealed in and cannot choose.

If I speak, death will steal my breath,
Seeping in at the mouth;
If I choose silence he may go away
And weep, and never know how close   10
My grave, how I longed to answer.

Someone flutes powder from my face.
I feel warm breath. My eyelids move:
Their flutter fills my eyes with grit.
Weight lifts from chest and arms   15
And inch by inch I live again.

In my father's arms
I cannot find strength to haul up
Words from my darkness.

by Angela Topping

Activities

① Read the poem above carefully and try to decide exactly what it is about.
You should pay particular attention to the way in which different emotions are
suggested by Angela Topping.

② Use the poem as the basis for a poem of your own, written from the father's viewpoint.
It should suggest the emotions he feels as he searches for, and eventually finds,
his buried child.

  a Begin by creating a list of words which could be used to describe the father's changing
  feelings as he digs through the rubble.

  b Try to use the structure of the poem above to suggest that what the father feels mirrors
  the feelings of his child. 📖

Case Study

What happened in the 1999 earthquake in Turkey?

*On Tuesday 17 August 1999 at 3 a.m. a strong earthquake hit north-west Turkey. Its epicentre was close to the city of Izmit, 55 km south-east of Istanbul (see map **A**).*

The information on pages 38–41 comes from a variety of sources written at different times over the months following the earthquake.

A The location of the earthquake

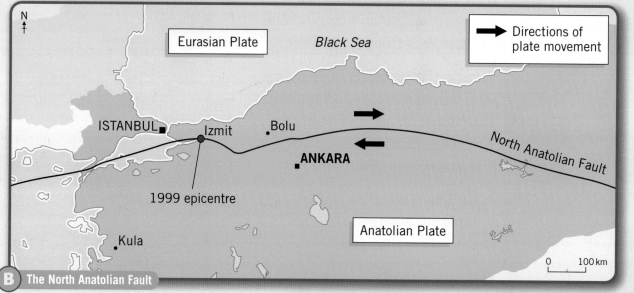

B The North Anatolian Fault

The earthquake's epicentre was about 11 km south-east of the city of Izmit. It was caused by the movement of the Eurasian Plate (moving east) and the Anatolian Plate (moving west) in an active zone known as the North Anatolian Fault (see map **B**). In places the plates moved up to 5 metres in opposite directions. The effects of this could be seen on roads and railways that crossed the North Anatolian Fault (see photo **D**).

The earthquake measured 7.4 on the Richter scale. It happened 17 km below the Earth's surface. Shallow earthquakes are often more powerful than deeper ones because there is less of the Earth's crust above them to absorb the force.

C Report from The National Earthquake Information Centre

D A railway crossing the North Anatolian Fault

Terror in Turkey: quake kills more than 2000

The worst recorded earthquake to hit Turkey killed at least 2000 people and injured thousands today. It destroyed buildings and cut off power and water to millions living in the area.

The quake struck at 3 a.m. this morning, catching most people asleep. The lucky ones ran into the street in panic; others were crushed in the rubble. Many fled their homes in nightclothes and without shoes. Later, they walked through the glass-strewn streets with cloth wrapped around their feet.

Dozens of buildings and highway overpasses collapsed in Istanbul, and many roads were severely damaged and unusable.

With the city's rescue services stretched to the limit, it was mostly neighbours and relatives who fought to pull people from the wreckage.

Local people working under car headlights in the early hours used their bare hands to try to dig people out of the rubble, while the young and elderly slept in the open.

Rescue teams with sniffer dogs and supplies have been sent from the United States, France, Germany, Switzerland, Italy, Japan and Israel, but hours after the quake, many victims still remain buried in the rubble of their homes.

Hospitals in Izmit have been turning away people with minor injuries and treating people on pavements. Medical workers have been breaking chemists' windows to get supplies.

E Newspaper report, 17 August 1999

Dead	Injured	People homeless	People living on the streets
15 135	23 983	600 000	200 000

F Casualty assessment report by Government Crisis Centre, 6 September 1999

Place	Date	Magnitude	Deaths
Turkey	1999	7.2	15 135
Afghanistan	1998	7.1	5000
Afghanistan	1998	6.4	4000
Iran	1997	7.1	1613
Russia	1995	7.5	1841
Japan	1995	7.2	6424
India	1993	6.4	7801
Indonesia	1992	6.8	2000
India	1991	6.1	1500
Afghanistan	1991	6.8	1500
Philippines	1990	7.7	1641
Iran	1990	7.7	40 000

G The worst earthquakes of the 1990s

I heard a deep thump and a few seconds later the whole house started shaking like crazy. We had a hard time running down the stairs, getting tossed from one side to the other. It did not stop for 45 seconds. When we reached the garden I saw the water in the swimming pool getting splashed around as if a ship was going through it. Tiles around the pool were shooting 1-2 metres up into the air. Then it stopped.

Minutes after the quake the entire city was without power. I saw a starry sky for the first time in more than a decade as the city was in total darkness, apart from the headlights of the cars driving around aimlessly ...

This is the first time I have ever felt so close to dying. You feel so helpless ... nothing you can do. Now I know that nothing is permanent in the world.

Kadir Bahcecik, Istanbul

H E-mail sent to a website for those wishing to contact family and friends after the earthquake

'I have been crying for two nights and no one has come to save my family,' shouted Mehmet, as he burst into the mayor's office with tears streaming down his face. 'If you don't come to my house soon, I will dynamite it myself to free them!' Anger, desperation and grief had carved deep lines around his mouth. He, like thousands of others, can't understand why there isn't a crane on every heap of rubble searching for those still missing.

I Television news report, 20 August 1999

SHODDILY BUILT HOUSES COLLAPSE IN QUAKE

There has been growing public anger that so many buildings fell down because precautions against earthquakes had not been taken.

In recent years, officials have turned a blind eye to builders who have skimped on materials to provide housing for the flood of people moving in from the countryside.

In the town of Duzce, 33 people thought to be responsible for the collapse of several buildings have been arrested. One of them admitted to mixing salty sea water with concrete. This caused buildings to crumble when the quake hit.

Buildings constructed over the past five years, using Turkey's earthquake building code, seem to have survived the quake much better.

J Newspaper report, 23 August 1999

40 000 FEARED DEAD IN TURKISH QUAKE

Fears are growing that the death toll from Turkey's devastating earthquake could eventually reach 40 000, making it the country's worst this century.

More than 10 000 people are already known to have died and another 45 000 people have been injured. The Turkish authorities are predicting that thousands more bodies will be found beneath the rubble.

Rescuers breaking iron bars to reach a trapped woman

Concern is growing for the health of those who have lived through the quake, with disease the latest threat to survivors. The fear of aftershocks has persuaded millions of people to camp out in the open – close to the rotting bodies of those killed in the earthquake. 'The greatest problem now facing us is that of disease,' Prime Minister Ecevit told reporters.

Most rescue workers are wearing masks, and are being immunised against typhoid. Cholera cases are being reported in some areas.

K Newspaper report, 20 August 1999

Houses damaged beyond repair
120 000
Houses heavily damaged
50 000
Other collapsed buildings
2000
Other heavily damaged buildings
4000

L Building damage assessment, as reported by Government Crisis Centre, 6 September 1999

The earthquake damaged buildings from Istanbul to Bolu (a distance of 250 km). Nearly 70 per cent of the buildings in the cities of Golcuk, Izmit, Topcular and Kular fell down. Most deaths and injuries were caused by collapsing buildings.

While most buildings were damaged by the shaking of the ground, on the coast waves rushed in as the ground sank and washed houses into the sea. Many of the collapsed buildings were four to eight storeys high and built of reinforced concrete.

Buildings collapsed as a result of:

- poor concrete quality
- poor reinforcement
- building alterations (e.g. an added floor)
- badly prepared building sites.

It will cost about £3.4 billion to rebuild the destroyed buildings.

M Report by the Earthquake Engineering Research Institute

Winter thoughts weigh heavily on the homeless

Ankle-deep in mud, in tent cities swamped by rain, homeless quake survivors wonder whether they will have a sturdy roof over their heads by winter, now just two months away. Unfortunately, the odds are against them – 600 000 people have been left homeless. Although the government has announced the building of 200 000 new homes, these will take up to three years to complete. People whose houses are declared safe have been asked to return home.

N Newspaper report, 27 August 1999

O Newspaper report, September 1999

NEW SYSTEMS CONSIDERED

Mindful of dangers from new quakes, Turkey has been considering new preparation measures. The *Milliyet* newspaper reported today that the government would spend £2 million on an early-warning system for Istanbul, a city of 12 million people.

It said the system would provide an early warning of shock waves, allow damaged buildings to be checked quickly, and help to prevent gas leaks that could cause fires.

Activities

1. Write a script for a five-minute television news report on '*Why did so many people die in the Turkish earthquake?*'. It is to be broadcast one month after the earthquake. Include sections of information about:

   - the *cause* of the earthquake
   - the *effects* of the earthquake (on the people and the places)
   - the *responses* of the government and emergency services to the earthquake
   - how the Turkish government plans to *prevent* so many deaths next time.

2. Begin each section of the report with an enquiry question. For example, the first section might start with:

   What was the cause of the Turkish earthquake of 1999?

3. Your report should also contain:

   - location maps at different scales, labelled with information about the earthquake
   - eye-catching graphs and diagrams showing relevant data
   - memorable images (such as photographs)
   - stories about 'real' people affected by the earthquake – these help to capture the imagination of the viewers.

help!

Good geographers:

- think carefully about the best ways of presenting information
- write information in their own words
- alter the way information is presented, e.g. change tables into graphs or maps
- annotate or label maps, photographs and diagrams
- carry out their own research into enquiry questions.

How can people make earthquakes less of a hazard?

Scientists still cannot say when or where an earthquake will strike. Successful earthquake **prediction** is very rare. A famous example was the Haicheng earthquake in China in 1976. Local people reported early-warning signs, so many people were persuaded to camp outside. When a quake measuring 7.3 on the Richter scale struck, very few people were killed. This success came from guessing correctly that an earthquake was likely to happen, and from local people taking the warnings seriously. In other parts of the world, even careful **monitoring** using seismographs has not helped. In San Francisco, USA, in 1989 and Kobe, Japan, in 1995, the quakes came without any real warning signs; in Kobe, thousands of people were killed.

In many parts of the world it is now possible to say how likely an earthquake might be. This means that people can plan to reduce the effects of earthquakes when they happen. Since 1900 nearly 3 million people have lost their lives in earthquakes. Most deaths are caused by falling bridges and buildings.

Case Study: USA

The Transamerica Pyramid in San Francisco was built to withstand earthquakes. When a magnitude 7.1 earthquake struck California in 1989 the top floors swayed more than 30 cm from side to side but the building was not damaged. No one was seriously injured.

A

Case Study: India

In rich *and* poor parts of the world, buildings are tested for their ability to survive earthquakes. In India, different types of houses were built on a concrete platform on wheels. This was shaken by a tractor to show which house would survive an earthquake best.

B

Case Study: Peru

The government has trained local people to build cheap and simple earthquake-proof buildings. The design shown in **C** is a rectangular house built of bamboo covered with mud. The roof is made of timber and thatch. The people are very poor, so it was important to use local materials with a long life. The bamboo and wooden frame is flexible, making it earthquake-resistant. The mud-covered walls rest on a low foundation to protect them from ground water.

Rectangular shape   Timber and thatch roo

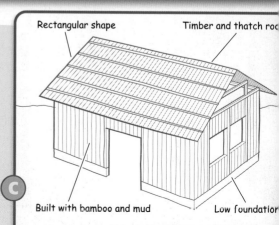

C

Built with bamboo and mud   Low foundatior

Case Study: West Coast, USA
Preparing an earthquake plan

- Choose a safe place in every room – under a table or against an inside wall where nothing can fall on you.

- Practise DROP, COVER, AND HOLD ON at least twice a year. Drop under a table, hold on, and protect your eyes.

- Find out ways you can protect your home, such as bolting the house to its foundation.

- Take a first-aid class.

- Train in how to use a fire extinguisher.

- Bolt bookcases, china cabinets and other tall furniture to the wall. Put strong latches on cupboards. Strap the water heater to the wall.

- Prepare a Disaster Kit for the home and car containing:

  – first-aid kit

  – canned food and can-opener

  – fifteen litres of water per person

  – protective clothing and sleeping-bags

  – radio, flashlight and batteries

  – written instructions for how to turn off gas, electricity and water.

D

Rich *and* poor countries carry out earthquake drills. These Californian schoolchildren are practising an earthquake drill.

F

Monitoring how structures behave

Scientists have put instruments into dams, bridges, pipelines, roads and buildings to monitor how they behave during earthquakes. The man in the photo below is checking earthquake monitoring equipment in California.

E

Activities

1. Locate the countries in the case studies on these two pages on an outline world map. Add an annotation box about each case study.

2. In each box describe what is being done and explain how this can help to reduce the effects of earthquakes.

3. The different ways of reducing the effects of earthquakes can be classified according to whether they involve:

   - educating people about what to do before, during or after an earthquake
   - improving buildings through better design and construction
   - monitoring earth movements.

   Shade the annotation boxes in three different colours according to which classification they match. Some boxes may require more than one colour.

4. Add a key and a title to your map.

5. **Extension**
   Find out about other case studies for different parts of the world.
   a Annotate the case studies onto your world map.
   b Colour the annotation boxes to classify each way of reducing earthquake effects.

How do people live with earthquakes and volcanoes?

Earthquakes may be inevitable, but some earthquake disasters are not. Scientists and engineers work to understand earthquake hazards. This helps people to prepare for future earthquakes, especially in active zones which are very densely populated. They can try to predict the earthquake, and reduce the damage by being better prepared.

How can earthquakes be predicted?

If scientists can predict when and where an earthquake will happen, people can be warned and lives saved, so scientists **monitor** active zones.

🜨 Sensitive instruments measure earth movements and check the strain building up in rocks.

🜨 The number of earthquakes can be plotted to show if a major earthquake is likely. Figure **A** shows that a major earthquake is expected around San Francisco Bay in the next thirty years.

🜨 Several earthquakes often strike in a short time. **Foreshocks** occur before some large earthquakes, so scientists can work out the chances of a larger **mainshock** following. In August 1989 a shock of magnitude 5.1 struck near San Francisco. The public was warned that a larger quake could follow. Sixty-nine days later, 63 people were killed by the Loma Prieta quake, magnitude 7.1.

🜨 Hazard shaking maps (see **B**) show the risk of earthquakes. They can help governments to plan emergency services and earthquake education. Engineers can plan earthquake codes for buildings, bridges and roads.

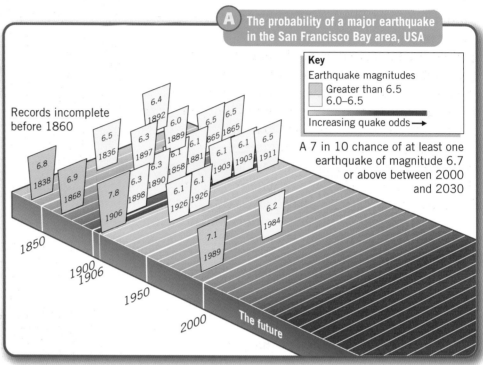

A The probability of a major earthquake in the San Francisco Bay area, USA

Key
Earthquake magnitudes
Greater than 6.5
6.0–6.5
Increasing quake odds ➝

A 7 in 10 chance of at least one earthquake of magnitude 6.7 or above between 2000 and 2030

Records incomplete before 1860

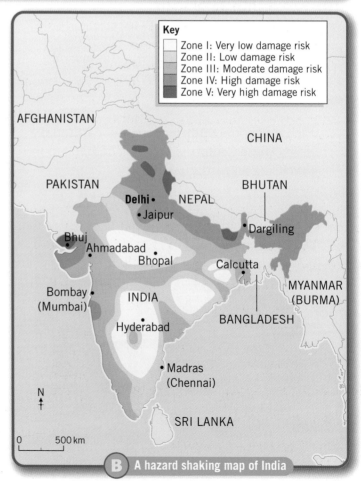

Key
Zone I: Very low damage risk
Zone II: Low damage risk
Zone III: Moderate damage risk
Zone IV: High damage risk
Zone V: Very high damage risk

B A hazard shaking map of India

How can people prepare for earthquakes?

Building codes

Many people are killed when earthquakes destroy buildings. Scientists can test how buildings respond to quakes, and improve their ability to survive, by using quake tables or platforms. The world's largest quake table is in Tsukuba Science City, Japan. It can carry buildings of up to 300 tonnes. Photo **B** on page 42 shows a smaller shake table being used to test houses in India. Houses are built on a platform mounted on rollers, which is shaken by a tractor. The building on the right of the photo, made with cement mortar, collapses but the other, built with mud mortar, survives.

Education

People in Japan practise earthquake drills every year on 'Disaster Day' – 1 September. Similar drills are carried out in other places where earthquakes are a hazard, for example by practising DROP, COVER, AND HOLD ON (enter code 5430P and follow the links to the Red Cross website at www.heinemann.co.uk/hotlinks).

Emergency services and relief

Governments must plan carefully to make sure the emergency services are prepared for possible earthquakes, and that relief supplies are ready. Good communication with earthquake monitoring stations can also save lives. This may be a problem for countries that cannot afford monitoring equipment and sophisticated communications.

C High, earthquake-proof buildings, Japan

Activities ICT

The information on pages 44 and 45 is about how people predict and prepare for earthquakes to try to reduce their effects. Carry out an Internet enquiry into how people predict and prepare for volcanic eruptions.

⑥ Answer the questions using the websites and links available at www.heinemann.co.uk/hotlinks using code 5430P.

⑥ Include case study information and illustrations.

How can volcanic eruptions be predicted?

❶ How can volcanoes be monitored?

❷ What signs suggest a volcano may soon erupt?

How can people prepare for volcanic eruptions?

❸ How are eruption warnings given?

❹ How can the public be better informed about volcanic hazards?

❺ What should people do if a volcano erupts?

help!

✪ Type the enquiry questions into a Word document.

✪ Copy and paste relevant information from the websites under each question.

✪ Highlight in red the most relevant information, then delete the rest.

✪ Put the text into a logical order.

✪ Insert side headings for each section of information.

How can aid help the victims of earthquakes and volcanoes?

One way of helping countries that have been affected by earthquakes or volcanic eruptions is to give them **aid**. Aid can be given in many different forms. Some of these are shown in **A**.

The **donor**, which gives the aid, is usually a rich country. The **recipient**, which receives the aid, is often a poorer country. Aid is one way for wealthy countries to help poorer countries.

There are two main types of aid:

Money to pay for supplies or rebuilding programmes, e.g. housing, roads, energy

Technology, e.g. heat-seeking equipment or computers to help manage the relief operations

Different forms of aid

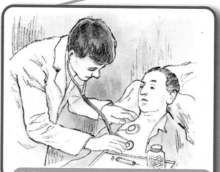

Skilled people, e.g. rescue workers, doctors and engineers, who can give advice and help people

Relief supplies: food, clothing, clean water, tents, planes and medical equipment

- **Official aid:** this is given by a government and paid for by the taxpayers of the donor country.

- **Voluntary aid:** this is provided by charities such as Oxfam, the Red Cross and Christian Aid.

Aid can be given in two ways:

- **Short-term emergency relief aid:** this is used to help solve immediate problems such as those caused by earthquakes, volcanic eruptions, floods or wars. It is sometimes called humanitarian aid.

- **Long-term development aid:** this gives people access to basic needs such as clean water and reliable food production. Long-term aid should help to improve living standards so that a country can develop.

Activities

1. At <u>heinemann.co.uk/hotlinks</u> enter code 5430P and follow the links for this page. For each charity you find there:

   a Write down its full name.

   b Name the recipient countries where the charity is providing aid at the moment.

   c Say whether it provides short-term aid. If so, list the types of disasters involved.

2. How do the charities differ in the forms of aid they provide?

B An American relief team's equipment arrives in Turkey

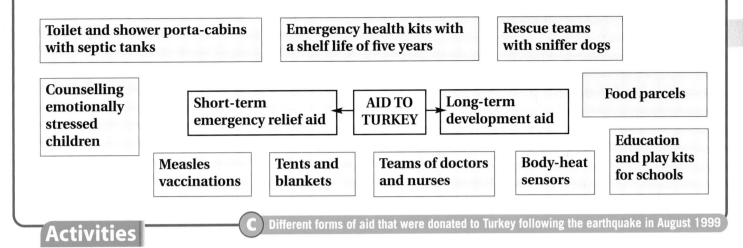

| Toilet and shower porta-cabins with septic tanks | Emergency health kits with a shelf life of five years | Rescue teams with sniffer dogs |

| Counselling emotionally stressed children | Short-term emergency relief aid | AID TO TURKEY | Long-term development aid | Food parcels |

| Measles vaccinations | Tents and blankets | Teams of doctors and nurses | Body-heat sensors | Education and play kits for schools |

C Different forms of aid that were donated to Turkey following the earthquake in August 1999

Activities

3 Make a copy of **C**. Draw an arrow from each example of aid in the pink boxes to either the short-term or the long-term aid box. If you think the example may be both short-term and long-term, draw an arrow to both blue boxes.

4 Compare your answers with one other person. Where you disagree, discuss the reasons for this.

Case Study

How has UNICEF provided aid for victims of the 1999 Turkish earthquakes?

UNICEF (United Nations Children's Fund) is a charity that supports children and helps to meet their basic needs. It aims to provide children with health care and food, clean water and education.

Seven months after the Izmit earthquake of August 1999 over 77 000 children under 8 were still homeless. Table **D** shows who donated money to UNICEF's long-term 'Recovery Plan for Turkish Children'. Table **E** shows you how the money was spent.

> **Where does UNICEF get its money from?**
>
> In 1998, 62 per cent of UNICEF's money came from the governments of different countries. The remaining 38 per cent came from fund-raising and the sale of greetings cards.

Groups that donated money	Amount donated (millions of US dollars)
Governments	7
UNICEF Committees	7.5
Total	14.5

D Money donated to UNICEF for the Turkish Recovery Plan

What money was spent on	Amount spent (millions of US dollars)
Water and sanitation	5
Education	4
Health	3
Emotional counselling	2.3
Transport	0.1
Children's play areas	0.1
Total	14.5

E How UNICEF spent aid money for the Recovery Plan

Activities

5 Draw two different types of graph to show the information on tables **D** and **E**. 📊

6 In what ways do your graphs show the information more clearly than the tables?

7 Which graph do you think shows the information best? Give reasons for your answer.

8 Why do you think UNICEF made water and sanitation its first priority?

9 Why might other charities have spent the money differently?

Adapted from: *UNICEF Recovery Plan for Turkish Children*, **13 March 2000**

Why do people choose to live in active zones?

A Geothermal energy (heat from the Earth) can be used to generate electrical power. This power station in Iceland also supplies the hot spring water for the local spa resort. Geothermal heat warms more than 70 per cent of homes in Iceland.

C This grid of fields is near Mount Aso in Japan. Over thousands of years, volcanic rocks have broken down to form some of the most fertile soils on Earth.

B Tourists are attracted to active zones to sightsee and to take part in activities. Here, in Lanzarote, tourists watch as a branch is set alight by the heat of the volcanic crater.

Activities

1 Draw a table like the one below.

Disadvantages of living in an active zone	Advantages of living in an active zone

2 Look through this chapter and complete the left-hand column of your table with the problems of living in active zones.

3 Read the information on this page and complete the right-hand column with the good points about living in active zones.

4 Look at the two lists you have written.

a Are there more advantages or more disadvantages?

b Do you think the disadvantages are more important than the advantages? If so, then why?

c Suggest problems in using only the information in this textbook to answer questions 2, 3 and 4.

5 Many people choose to live in an active zone even though it can be extremely hazardous. Why do you think this is the case?

My family has lived on the slopes of Mount Etna for many generations. We are prepared to live with the danger because we love it here ... it is our home.

D

Review and reflect

Key enquiry questions	Page numbers	Case Studies	What I learned about or did
What do you already know about earthquakes and volcanoes?	20, 21		Cause and effect
Where do volcanoes and earthquakes occur?	22, 23		Located features on a map
Why do volcanoes and earthquakes occur where they do?	24		Compared patterns on two maps
What are volcanoes?	25, 26, 27		Created a wordscape; Internet enquiry
What happens when a volcano erupts?	28, 29, 30, 31	Mount Pinatubo, Philippines	Annotated a map and cross-section
What are earthquakes? Are they all identical?	32, 33	Gujarat, India	Produced an earthquake case study
What happens in an earthquake?	34, 35		Researched using the Internet
How do earthquakes affect people and places?	36, 37		Explained how earthquakes affect people's lives
What happened in the 1999 earthquake in Turkey?	34, 35, 36, 37 38, 39, 40, 41	Izmit, Turkey	Researched an enquiry question
How can people make earthquakes less of a hazard?	42, 43		Described and explained
How do people live with earthquakes and volcanoes?	44, 45		Carried out an Internet enquiry
How can aid help the victims of earthquakes and volcanoes?	46, 47		Classified information
Why do people choose to live in active zones?	48		Identified problems from writing and photographs

Activities

1. Make a large copy of the table above. For each enquiry question, look back at your work for this unit and write down the names of the places you have studied in the 'Case Studies' column. Some have already been done to help you.

2. The fourth column gives at least one thing you should have learned about or done for each enquiry question. For each one, find where in your work you actually did this. Then add at least one more thing you learned. Some extra examples have been provided in the help box.

3. Write down the three most important things you have learned from your work on the Restless Earth. Explain why you chose them.

4. Write down three things you did or learned that might be useful in other subject areas. For example, writing a report would be useful in a history lesson.

5. Write down which activities you found most difficult. Give reasons for your choices.

help!

These ideas may help you to answer question **2**.

- Classification
- Research
- Writing in report genre
- Writing in recount genre
- Asking geographical questions
- Using an atlas
- Drawing graphs
- Working with others.

3 Rivers

A The Niagara Falls in North America

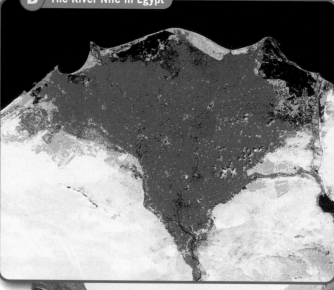

B The River Nile in Egypt

D The River Yangtse in China

C The Kariba dam in Zimbabwe

Learn about

Rivers are important to people because they provide water, are used for transport and can be used to provide power. Rivers are constantly changing the shape of the landscape. From the *source* of the river to its *mouth*, the features of a river and its valley change significantly. In this unit you will learn about:

- locating a river section you are going to study
- what you need to find out when you study rivers
- what information you can collect in the field
- what the collected data means
- what conclusions you can draw.

E The River Amazon in Brazil

F The River Forth estuary in Scotland

G A wedding party is escorted across flooded roads in North Yorkshire, England, 2000

H The Ganges in India is a sacred river for Hindus

I Transport on the River Nile, Egypt

J Lower Falls, Colorado River, USA

Getting Technical ▼

- ⑥ **Erosion** – wearing away the land and transporting the worn material away. This may be **vertical** or **horizontal** erosion in a river valley.

- ⑥ **Deposition** – laying down eroded material

- ⑥ **Weathering** – breaking down rock by exposure to weather conditions such as extreme heating or cooling, rainwater containing acid or biological activity. The rock is not transported away.

- ⑥ **Source** – the beginning of a river

- ⑥ **Waterfall** – a sharp break in the gradient of a river valley where water falls vertically

- ⑥ **Gorge** – a steep-sided, almost vertical, valley cut by a river

- ⑥ **Meanders** – a series of large sweeping bends in a river

- ⑥ **Delta** – where a river splits into several parts before it meets the sea

- ⑥ **Estuary** – where a river widens out in a funnel shape before it reaches the sea

Activities

1 Look carefully at the photographs on these two pages. Pick out the photographs where people are making use of rivers. Give a brief description of what the river is being used for in each photograph. 📖

2 **a** Select the photographs which show examples of the following river landscape features:

  i meanders **ii** waterfall **iii** gorge
  iv delta   **v** estuary.

b Using other sources of information, find out how any three of the river features are created. You can draw diagrams and use the words in the Getting Technical box to help you.

3 Start to make your own word bank of the key words in this unit. 📖

What do you already know about river patterns and processes?

Some of the main patterns and processes found in a river that has its source in a highland area are shown in **A**. Sometimes a river has its source in a lowland area.

A The long profile of a river

A river's source is often in highland areas where there is usually more rainfall and surface run-off water.

Upper course

250 m
200 m
150 m

Upland valley

V-shaped valley, the Scottish borders

Rocks and soil from the banks and valley sides may be broken down by weathering.

Middle section

100 m

150 m
100 m
50 m

Mid-section of a river in the UK

The river runs downstream from its source, cutting down its valley by **vertical erosion**. Valley sides are steep and there are usually large rocks on the river bed. Waterfalls are often found in this section. (See **B**)

The **gradient** of the river is gentler here and the channel is wider. Tributaries, surface run-off and ground water have increased the volume of the river. There is less vertical erosion and more lateral erosion.

Height (metres above sea level)

Length of river from source to mouth

Gradient or slope decreases

Average speed of the river increases

Size of the river increases

Size of the rocks on the bed of the river decreases

More vertical erosion → More lateral erosion

B Waterfall in Swinner Gill, Swaledale

Activities

1. Study the information about the long profile of a river in **A**. Imagine that you were following the river from its source to its mouth (from left to right in **A**). Write a description of the main changes that you would expect to see in the river and its valley. You could use the writing frame below to help start you off.

The start of a river or its _____ is usually in _____ because _____ . The main features of the river valley at this point include _____ . As the river flows downstream, the gradient becomes _____ . The next section is called the _____ of the river. At this point the river changes and becomes _____ .

Lower course or flood plain

Meandering River Tay, Scotland

The river is usually wider and deeper here. There is more lateral erosion where the river cuts wide sweeping bends or meanders.

2. Look at the annotated sketch **C** of the photograph of the upper course of the river. Draw a similar sketch of the photographs showing the middle section and lower course. Label or annotate the sketches to show the main features you would expect to find in each section of the river.

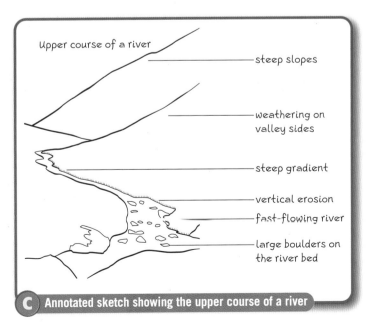

C Annotated sketch showing the upper course of a river

Getting Technical ▼

Rivers wear away or **erode** the land they flow over. This is called **fluvial erosion**. A river may erode its channel vertically (downwards) or **laterally** (sideways).

Where is the river section you are going to study?

Using contour lines to identify features in a river valley

You can use an Ordnance Survey (OS) map to identify detailed features in a river valley. The pattern of the contour lines shows the changes in the shape and gradient of the river valley and the surrounding area.

Map **A** is an OS map showing the river landscapes around the settlement of Dufftown in the Grampian mountains.

Road follows the flat section at the foot of the steep valley side.

The shape and pattern of the contour lines show a hill at 552m with steep slopes all around. Ideal in the past for a 'fort'.

Contour lines form a 'V' pattern around the smaller tributary rivers. This indicates a steep gradient and steep valley sides, so the valley has a V-shaped profile.

Contour lines are widely spaced, showing the river has a gentle slope.

Dullan Water meandering in the wide, flat valley floor.

Some smaller rivers and streams cut straight across the contour lines. This shows a very steep fall, usually a waterfall.

Contour lines are close together, showing a steep slope on the valley sides.

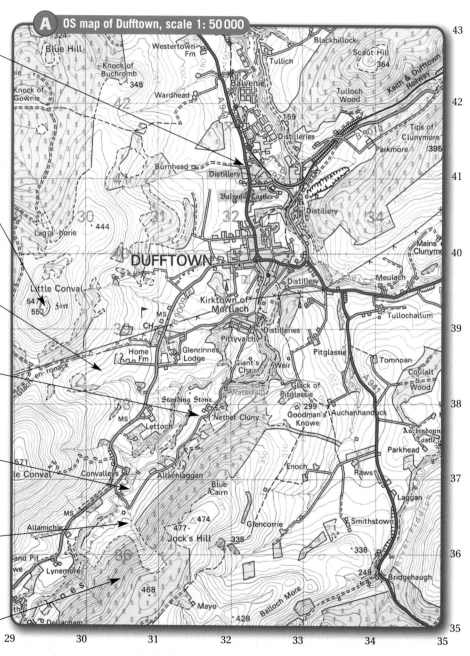

A OS map of Dufftown, scale 1: 50 000

© Crown copyright. Licence no. 100000 230

Drawing cross-sections from contour lines

Diagram **B** shows how the contour patterns drawn on an
OS map help you to identify what the landscape actually looks
like. Cross-sections taken across the contour lines show a
two-dimensional model of the landscape.

B Contour pattern and cross-section of a
steep-sided hill. The cross-section is taken
from grid reference 300360 to 320360 (A to B)

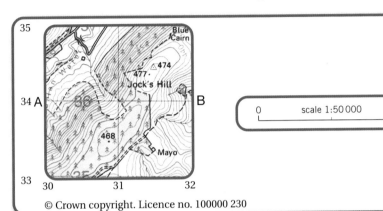

© Crown copyright. Licence no. 100000 230

scale 1:50 000

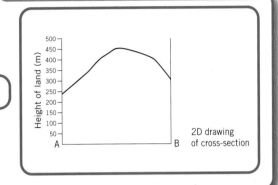

How to...

... draw a cross-section

When you draw a cross-section, you are imagining that
the land has been cut through to sea level and drawing
a two-dimensional image or side profile of what the
land looks like. Work through these four steps.

1 Place a strip of paper
   across the contour lines
   on the map where you
   want to take your section.

2 Mark the points where the
   contour lines cross the
   paper and write the height
   of each contour beside it.

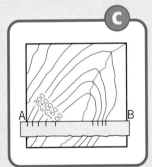

3 Take the paper off the map
   and use graph paper to
   construct the cross-
   section. The length of
   the cross-section forms
   the length of the bottom
   axis. Put sea level (0
   metres) at the bottom of
   the side axis, then draw
   a scale that can fit in the
   heights you have marked on your cross-section.

4 You may want to label the cross-section with the
   landscape features identified on the map.

Activities

1 **a** Draw a scaled cross-section of part of a river valley from a suitable place on OS map **A**.

   b Label your cross-section using the following terms:

   river   flat/steep valley sides

   c Add a heading and a scale to your cross-section.

2 **Extension**
   Choose a place on map **A** with a different shape of valley and draw a
   cross-section to represent it. Label your drawing and add a heading.

Investigating rivers: what do you need to find out?

You have discovered in this unit that:

⊚ rivers are constantly changing the landscape by a process called fluvial erosion

⊚ different landscape features and processes are found at different places in a river's valley.

A fieldwork investigation on a stretch of river would give you the chance to test what you already know and to find out more about rivers.

Step 1: Asking questions

The first step in a geography fieldwork investigation is to ask questions.
What do you want to find out about rivers? Your title for this investigation could be:

How do landscapes and processes change in a river valley?

Here are some of the questions you could use to investigate the changes.

| Do river valleys become wider further downstream? | Does the volume of water in a river increase further downstream? | Does the size of material in the river bed change as a river moves downstream? |

On which side of a meander bend does the river flow fastest?

Is there any evidence of erosion and deposition on a meander section?

Is the height of the bank above the river greater in some sections than in others?

A Measuring a stream for geography fieldwork

Is the deepest part of the river in the middle?

Does the river flow faster in the upper valley section or in the lower section?

Is the gradient of a river valley steeper in its upper course or in its lower course?

Activity

① In a group, study the enquiry questions above and decide which you are going to investigate. Then discuss what data you need and how you are going to collect it.

help!

It is better to work in a group because it makes data collection easier and safer. You must be sure to listen to advice about safety before you collect data in the field.

What information can you gather in the field?

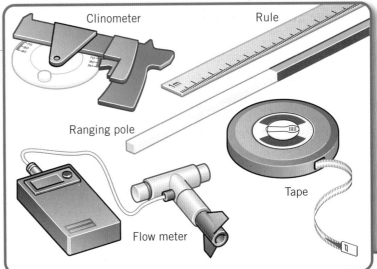

Step 2: Gathering information

First, decide which questions you are going to investigate. You may add a few more, but they must be relevant to your study. Now decide how you are going to gather the information. It is important to measure and record your data accurately.

◎ Most of the data you gather during a river investigation will be *primary data*, that is, data you actually go out and collect through measuring, sketching and observing.

◎ You could gather *secondary data* about the river you are investigating by contacting the Environment Agency. Find the link to their website by using www.heinemann.co.uk/hotlinks and entering code 5430P. You could then compare this secondary data with your own data.

How to ...

... record data

Before you go on your field trip, you need to construct data collection sheets to record your data accurately. Here is an example of a data collection sheet used to investigate channel depth across a stretch of river. The group decided to record the depth of the river at three or more different sites in the river valley by taking six depth readings at regular intervals across the river.

Position	Depth of river					
	Readings (cm) (starting on left bank)					
	1	2	3	4	5	6
Site 1	3.5	8	8.5	10	4	2.5
Site 2						

A Useful equipment for a river investigation

Activity

❶ In your group, decide what information you need to collect for each of the questions you are going to investigate. Construct data collection sheets for each investigation. (ICT) (123)

What does your data mean?

Step 3: Showing your results

Once you have gathered your data, you can start to write up your investigation and show what the data means. You will have gathered a lot of measurements at different points along the river. You can use some of these to draw cross-sections of the river channel. You can also work out the speed of flow and the changes in volume, processes and landforms as you move to different sections of the river. Use a variety of maps, labelled sketches, photographs, cross-sections, graphs and written work to show this information. Look at the next four pages to discover new techniques for analysing and presenting your data.

Drawing a field sketch

When you were out gathering your data you may have sketched the river valley at different locations. You can now draw neater versions of your field sketches and annotate them to highlight the main features and processes. You can see a sketch and sketch plan that a student drew as part of her investigation in **A** and **B**. If you have taken images with a digital camera, you could load them onto a PC, annotate them and print them off to add to your investigation.

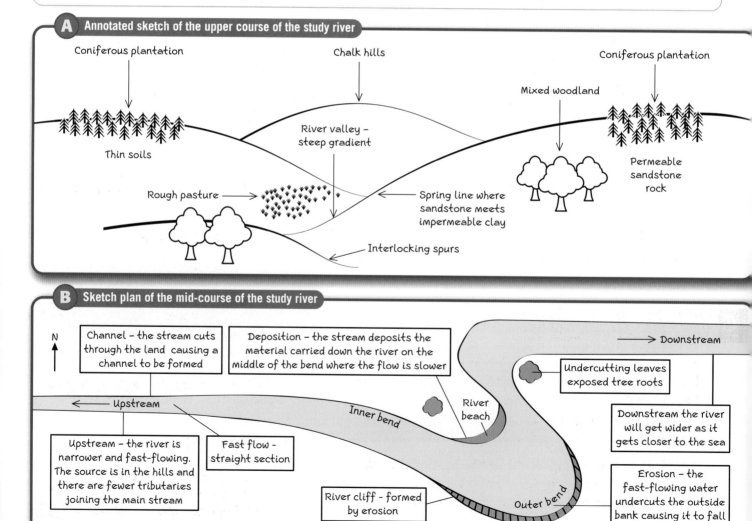

A Annotated sketch of the upper course of the study river

Coniferous plantation

Chalk hills

Coniferous plantation

Mixed woodland

Thin soils

River valley – steep gradient

Permeable sandstone rock

Rough pasture

Spring line where sandstone meets impermeable clay

Interlocking spurs

B Sketch plan of the mid-course of the study river

N

Channel – the stream cuts through the land causing a channel to be formed

Deposition – the stream deposits the material carried down the river on the middle of the bend where the flow is slower

Downstream

Undercutting leaves exposed tree roots

Upstream

Inner bend

River beach

Downstream the river will get wider as it gets closer to the sea

Upstream – the river is narrower and fast-flowing. The source is in the hills and there are fewer tributaries joining the main stream

Fast flow – straight section

River cliff – formed by erosion

Outer bend

Erosion – the fast-flowing water undercuts the outside bank causing it to fall

Drawing cross-sections

To draw the cross-section of a river, you need measurements of:

- ◎ the depth of the river
- ◎ the width of the channel
- ◎ the width of the river from bank to bank
- ◎ the height of the bank above the river.

How to ...

... draw a cross-section of a river

1 Look at the measurements you have gathered and decide on a scale that will fit on your paper.

2 Start your section by drawing the width of the river. Make sure that you have enough room to draw in the river channel below it.

3 Look at the measurements for the height of the bank above the river level on both sides and mark in the position of both banks.

4 Measure the width of the channel bank to bank. Now draw in the banks.

5 Next you can mark in the river bed by using the measurements of the depth of the river from the surface and marking the points on the cross-section. Join the points together to show the river bed.

6 Add a scale and a heading.

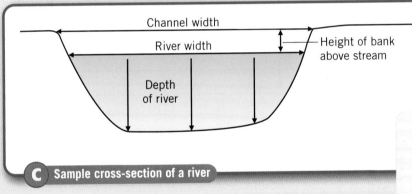

C **Sample cross-section of a river**

Width of channel from bank to bank: 155 cm

Width of river: 120 cm

Height of bank above the river:
  left side: 25 cm
  right side: 53 cm

Depth of river:

	Left bank			Right bank
Reading	1	2	3	4
Depth (cm)	12	31	35	10

D **Readings at a cross-section of a river**

Getting Technical ▼

◎ The amount of water flowing down a stream is known as the **discharge**. The discharge can be calculated by using this formula:

  discharge = velocity × area

◎ To work out the area of a cross-section of a river:

1 Calculate the average depth by adding all the depth readings and divide by the number of readings. In **D** the average would be (12 + 31 + 35 + 10)/4 = 22 cm.

2 Multiply the average depth by the average width of the river to give the area. In **D** the area would be 22 × 120 = 2640 cm².

Activity

❶ The figures in **D** are taken from a different section of the river shown in **C** below. Draw a cross-section by following the steps carefully. ①②③

Drawing long profiles and graphs

You can show many of the changes you recorded in your fieldwork by drawing a long profile of the river you have been studying. This long profile will help you to make a summary of your investigation. Follow the steps in the How to ... box to draw your own long profile.

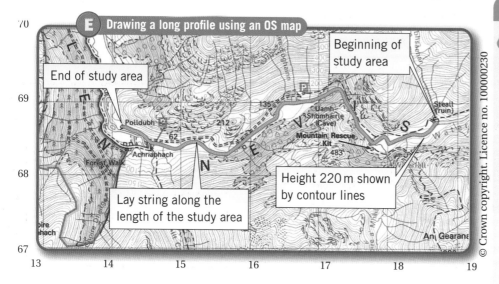

E Drawing a long profile using an OS map

End of study area

Beginning of study area

Lay string along the length of the study area

Height 220 m shown by contour lines

© Crown copyright. Licence no. 100000230

Activity

2 Using a suitable OS map, find a section of a river where you can see clear differences in height and changes in its features. You could use map **A** on page 54. Draw a long profile of the section using the instructions in the How to ... box. Mark on your profile any changes you can see on the map. Look for evidence of the contour patterns showing valley width or steepness, or features such as waterfalls and bridges.

How to ...

... draw a long profile

You will need an OS map of the section of river you were investigating.

1 Use a piece of string to measure the length of the section of river you were investigating on the map. This will be the length of the long profile for the horizontal axis.

2 Estimate the height of the river where your study started by looking for evidence of spot heights or contour lines on the map. Now look for the height of the point where your study finished. The difference between these two

heights will give you the height of your profile for the vertical axis.

3 Now place a straight edge of paper along the length of the river and carefully mark each point where the river crosses a contour line. Write the height of the contour line beside your mark. Put your paper along the bottom of the profile. Mark off changes in height. Join up the points to draw your profile.

4 Label the profile with the information you have collected at your three study sites, including the measurements and main features. You could use photos, sketches or cross-sections.

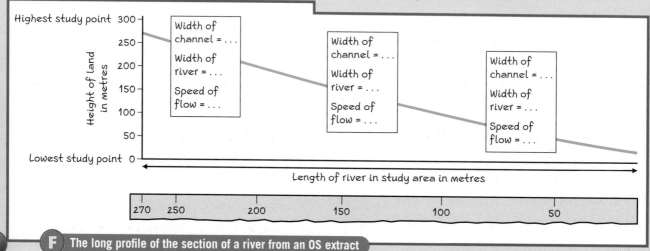

F The long profile of the section of a river from an OS extract

Graphs and proportional lines

Some of the data you have collected may be difficult to show well in a profile or a sketch. It may be better to show it by drawing graphs or proportional lines. Examples of such data include:

⊚ the speed of flow, or **velocity**, in different sections of the river

⊚ the size and shape of bed material found in different sections

⊚ changes in velocity across the river (see **G** below).

Look at **G** to see how a set of data can be shown in two different ways.

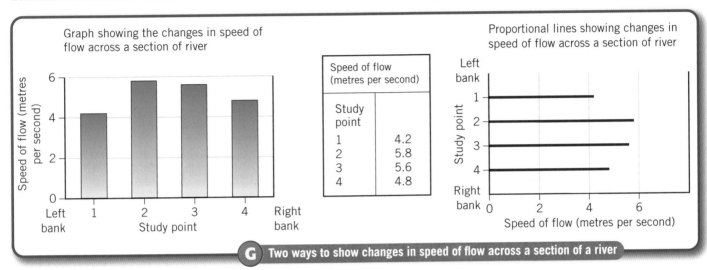

G Two ways to show changes in speed of flow across a section of a river

Activities

❸ Some students from the Deepings School measured the velocity of the Winceby Beck at five points down its length. They took three readings at each point. Copy out their results in the table below, and work out the average speed of flow at each of the five river study points. (123)

Study points along the river's course:						
Nearest the source	1	2	3	4	5	Nearest the mouth
Velocity (m/sec)						
Reading 1	4.2	3.4	3.1	5.2	6.3	Reading 1
Reading 2	4.8	4.0	2.9	5.0	5.5	Reading 2
Reading 3	4.0	3.8	3.5	4.1	6.1	Reading 3
Average						

❹ Now draw a graph or proportional lines to show how the speed of flow changes along the course of the river. You might like to use a spreadsheet package to draw the graph. (123) (ICT)

❺ Look at the graph or lines you have drawn for question **4** and write a comment about what is shown. You may use the following writing frame to start you off. 📖

> **Comment on the changes in speed of flow along a river's profile**
>
> The fastest flowing section of the river is at study point _____ , recording an average speed of _____ metres/sec. The slowest section is at study point _____ which records an average speed of _____ metres/sec.
>
> This shows that ...
>
> The reason for this pattern/result may be ...

Step 4: Drawing conclusions

Once you have gathered enough data and displayed the results using a range of techniques, you must now draw some conclusions about your investigation and evaluate your work. The more data you gather, the more reliable your conclusions will be.

help!

A conclusion:

- looks at all the work you have done
- links the results to the questions you asked in the beginning.

An evaluation:

- looks at the strengths and the weaknesses of the work as a whole
- makes suggestions about further investigations you might carry out.

Conclusion

The main enquiry question was:

How do landscapes and processes change in a river valley?

The first part of your conclusion should give a general statement about what you found from your investigations. You could start your conclusion by writing:

> From my study of the different sections of the river … I found that the river landscapes and processes did change as it moved downstream. The main changes were …

Now give details including figures and refer to the diagrams, maps and graphs you have drawn.

Evaluation

Your evaluation should finish off your enquiry. It refers to the whole piece of work and you should make a note of the strengths and weaknesses of the project. You should mention what went well and what didn't go so well. Go on to suggest how it could be improved next time. You also need to suggest ideas for further investigation of the same topic.

You could start your evaluation by writing:

> I learned a lot about river landscapes and processes from doing this enquiry. I also learned how important it was to …

You could then go on to say:

> We had some difficulty gathering the information because …

and finally give suggestions of how you could extend your investigations:

> It would be good to go and do some further study on …

Activity

6 Now that you have learned to gather primary data, used different methods of presenting your data, drawn conclusions and evaluated your work, you can write an investigation using secondary data. You could, for example, use data from the Environment Agency's website (see page 57). You should try to get information for a complete stretch of river rather than just the two or three sections that you studied in your fieldwork. ICT 📖 123

Review and reflect

Activities

1 **a** In this unit you have learned about river valley processes, landscape patterns and how to complete a fieldwork investigation. Complete a spider diagram like the one below to make a summary of the facts you have learned while studying this section. Add any further relevant facts, including details from your fieldwork.

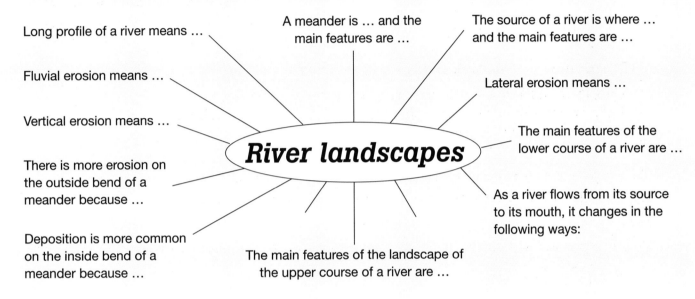

Long profile of a river means …

A meander is … and the main features are …

The source of a river is where … and the main features are …

Fluvial erosion means …

Lateral erosion means …

Vertical erosion means …

River landscapes

The main features of the lower course of a river are …

There is more erosion on the outside bend of a meander because …

As a river flows from its source to its mouth, it changes in the following ways:

Deposition is more common on the inside bend of a meander because …

The main features of the landscape of the upper course of a river are …

b Use the terms in your spider diagram to start a geography word bank.

2 Now you have learned to carry out a fieldwork enquiry on a river landscape you will be able to apply the same skills to any other enquiry by using these steps:

○ **Deciding on a title** – this is often in the form of a question, which may start with the words:

What is …? Where are …? How …? Who …? Why …?

It may also state a **hypothesis** (a theory) which you set out to prove or disprove through your investigation.

○ **Gathering information** – you must decide what information you need and where you can get it, and design data collection sheets. Look back at page 57 to remind you.

○ **Showing results** – you can use many different methods to show your results: maps, graphs, sketches, photographs, written work. You can see examples on pages 58–61.

○ **Drawing conclusions and evaluating** – you must reflect back to the original title of your study and attempt to answer it using evidence from the data you have collected. Look back at page 62.

Position	Depth of river					
	Readings (cm) (starting on left bank)					
	1	2	3	4	5	6
Site 1	3.5	8	8.5	10	4	2.5
Site 2						

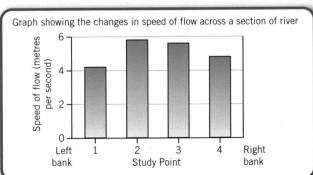

Graph showing the changes in speed of flow across a section of river

4 Coastal environments

A Cliff erosion in Great Cowden near Hornsea, England

Learn about

The Earth's scenery or landscape varies from place to place and is changing all the time. Knowing and understanding about the processes that cause these changes can help people manage the problems they can create. In this unit you will learn:

⊚ how weathering and erosion affect coastlines

⊚ how the coast is shaped by the sea in different ways

⊚ what causes some parts of the coast to collapse

⊚ how people try to manage the coast by protecting it against the sea.

Activity

❶ Write down five geographical questions you could ask someone about the scene in photograph **A**. Think of questions that would help you to find out how this farm on top of a cliff has been destroyed. Use words like *why, where, what* and *how* in your questions.

How is our coastline formed?

The UK's coastline stretches for over 10 000 kilometres around the country. It attracts millions of people, both for its wild and natural beauty and its sandy beaches and exciting nightlife. Coasts change rapidly – they are dynamic places – and the natural processes of **weathering** and **erosion** are acting on the rocks along the coast all the time to shape it into the bays, beaches and **headlands** that people like to visit. How does this happen?

What is weathering?

The landscapes of the world are constantly changing. Rain, sun, wind and frost are breaking down even the hardest rocks into smaller pieces before they are carried away. This process is known as weathering. There are three main types of weathering.

Mechanical weathering is caused by changes in temperature. In freeze–thaw weathering, water gets into cracks in a rock and freezes. As it freezes it expands. Repeated freezing and melting eventually cause the rock to split.

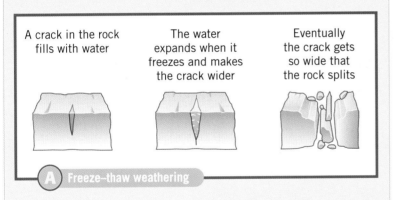

| A crack in the rock fills with water | The water expands when it freezes and makes the crack wider | Eventually the crack gets so wide that the rock splits |

A Freeze–thaw weathering

Biological weathering is caused by the action of plants on rocks. Plants can grow in cracks in rocks. As their roots develop they can force the cracks to widen and the rocks to fall apart. Lichens and mosses can also grow on rocks. They make the rock surface slowly crumble.

C Biological weathering in Majorca, Spain

Chemical weathering is caused by the action of water on the chemicals in rock. Rainwater is made slightly acidic as it falls through the atmosphere. When it comes into contact with rock, it dissolves some of it away. Chemical weathering is most effective in warm, wet areas. To find more information on how chemical weathering affects limestone, go to www.heinemann/hotlinks and enter code 5430P. Sea water can also cause chemical weathering.

B The cracks in this limestone pavement are caused by chemical weathering

Activities

1. Write a sentence to describe what *weathering* means.

2. Draw a set of diagrams like those in **A** to describe how biological weathering occurs.

3. Put these sentences in order to describe how chemical weathering occurs.

   ⑥ The weakly acidic rainwater attacks the rock.

   ⑥ Rainwater becomes acid as it falls through the atmosphere.

   ⑥ The rock dissolves and crumbles away.

4. Carry out a survey of your own school to find out where the building is being weathered. Think of some enquiry questions you could ask about where the weathering is found, e.g. how high up or on which side of the building it is.

What is erosion?

Getting Technical ▼

Weathering is a process that weakens and breaks up rocks. The wearing away of the rocks and the removal of the weathered material is called **erosion**. The loose weathered material can be carried away by rivers, wind, the sea, ice – or by people. The work of these **agents of erosion** is explained below.

Rivers are constantly wearing away tiny pieces of rock from their banks and their beds. These particles are carried away by the river. When a river is in flood it can carry huge boulders.

A River erosion, the Falls of Clyde, Scotland

B The Mittens in Arizona, USA

If you walk along a beach when there is a strong **wind**, you will feel the sand blowing against your face. The particles carried by the wind blast away the rocks in their path, sometimes forming weird and wonderful shapes like this.

C Waves erode the cliffs on the Oregon coast, USA

Waves constantly batter our shores and wear away the cliffs. Eroded particles are carried away by the waves or by currents and are deposited on beaches. Material can also be moved along beaches by waves.

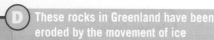
D These rocks in Greenland have been eroded by the movement of ice

In mountain and polar regions, huge masses of **ice** move down valleys and across plains. As they travel, they pick up rocks and stones which grind away at the ground surface below, wearing down the land like sandpaper. The material they move collects in huge mounds at the end of the valley.

E This footpath on Ben Nevis, Scotland, has been eroded by millions of feet

People cause erosion in many different ways. Bulldozers can be used to dig out large amounts of soil. People can wear away a surface just by walking over it. They can also remove trees and other plants which hold the soil together, allowing water and wind to remove the soil more easily.

Washing the dishes is like erosion. The force of the water and the scrubbing you do remove the dirt from the plates. Throwing the water away **transports** the waste material down the drain to another place, where it is **deposited**. On a larger scale, mountains, valleys and coasts are shaped and changed by water, wind and ice. Erosion wears away the land; the loose material is transported to another place where it may be deposited to make new landforms.

I'm just eroding the dishes!

Activities

1 **a** Write two or three sentences to explain the difference between weathering and erosion. Use words like *breaking down*, *transportation* and *wearing away*.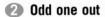

   b Add the words *erosion* and *weathering* to your word bank.

2 **Odd one out**

1 Freeze–thaw	5 Transport	9 River
2 Weathering	6 Mechanical	10 People
3 Biological	7 Deposit	11 Tree roots
4 Wind	8 Erosion	12 Glacier

For each set below, decide which is the odd one out, and give a reason for your choice.

Set A	1	2	9	**Set D**	11	7	3
Set B	2	7	6	**Set E**	4	5	11
Set C	5	9	12	**Set F**	7	8	10

3 **Extension**

Which of the following groups of people would find weathering a positive thing? Which would find it a negative thing? Explain your answers.

House-owners　　**Farmers**　　**Architects**

4 Make your own scale of hardness using things you can find at home. Test five materials by trying to scratch them with a nail file or emery board. You could include glass, steel, concrete or wax. Complete a table of your results.

Scale of hardness	Material
Hardest 1	
2	
3	
4	
Softest 5	

Hard and soft rocks

The rate at which rocks are weathered and eroded has a lot to do with how hard they are. Some rocks are soft – they crumble easily in your hands or they are washed away very easily, for example **clay** or **chalk**. Other rocks are made of particles or crystals which are very hard or which are cemented together to make them very resistant to erosion. Rocks like this include **granite** and **marble**.

How do waves shape our coast?

Waves are responsible for most of the landforms we see on our coasts. They are eroding the land and moving material all day and all night. But most erosion happens on stormy days when strong winds drive large waves against the shore. These waves have such force that they can break off bits of rocks from cliffs and move vast amounts of sand and shingle from one place to another. The sea erodes the land, transports the eroded material and deposits it elsewhere. A series of coastal landforms are created, some of them by erosion, some by deposition.

A Kiloran Bay on Colonsay, Scotland

D Aerial view of Chesil Beach, Dorset, England

B Vertical cliffs of the Seven Sisters, East Sussex, England

E Mount Cliff, Beaumaris, Wales

C Country Park, East Lothian, Scotland showing saltmarsh, sandflats and spits

Activities

1. Look at photographs **A–E**. Put them into pairs and look for connections between them. For example, **A** and **B** both show cliffs. There is more than one correct answer – your answer is right as long as you have found a good connection.

2. Copy the table below. Write down the letters for each of your pairs with a short explanation of the connection.

Pair	Connection
A and B	Both show cliffs

How does the sea erode the coast?

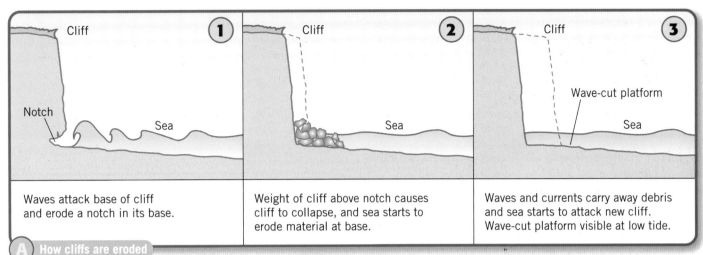

Waves attack base of cliff and erode a notch in its base.	Weight of cliff above notch causes cliff to collapse, and sea starts to erode material at base.	Waves and currents carry away debris and sea starts to attack new cliff. Wave-cut platform visible at low tide.

A How cliffs are eroded

Erosion occurs in different ways along the coast when powerful waves crash against the foot of a cliff.

- The waves hurl sand and shingle against the cliff. This scrapes at the rocks on the cliff, rather like sandpaper.

- Waves also trap air in the cracks in the rock, and the pressure created causes large pieces of rock to break off.

Softer rocks are eroded more easily and wear away more quickly forming bays. Harder rocks form cliffs and stand out as headlands. Photograph **B** shows what happens when bands of hard and soft rock reach the coast.

How to ...

... describe a photograph of a coastline

1 Begin with a general statement, e.g. *The picture shows a coast with bays and headlands.*

2 Go on to give greater detail about the type of rock you can see, the colours and the shapes that they make. Use words like *vertical*, *angular*, *rounded*.

3 Mention whether the rock is bare or covered in vegetation. Is there any sign of people or their activities?

4 Try to find something in the picture to give you a scale and try to give sizes to what you are describing.

B This coastline in Pembrokeshire, Wales, is formed of hard and soft bands of rock

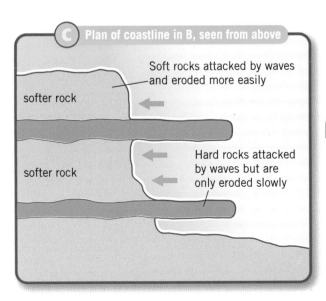

C Plan of coastline in B, seen from above

Soft rocks attacked by waves and eroded more easily

softer rock

softer rock

Hard rocks attacked by waves but are only eroded slowly

Activities

1 Make a list of words that would help you describe the coast in photograph **B**.

2 Use your list and the How to ... box to help you write a description of the coast in the photograph.

3 Use diagram **C** to help you explain how the headlands and bays in **B** were formed. You may need to draw a series of diagrams like diagram **C** to show changes over time.

D Erosion of a headland

1

2

3

E A cave, an arch and a stack at Elegug, Wales

Activities

④ The three diagrams in **D** show how the sea erodes cliffs to develop other landforms (see **E**). Make a sketch of the photo and then use the labels below to annotate your diagrams.

- ⊚ The sea attacks small cracks and opens them.
- ⊚ The cracks get larger and develop into a small **cave**.
- ⊚ When the cave wears right through the headland, an **arch** forms.
- ⊚ More erosion causes the arch to collapse. This leaves a pillar of rock called a **stack** in the sea.

⑤ Map **F** shows that the area is made up of several different types of rocks, which are shown in the key.

- **a** Trace or draw a sketch map of the coast.
- **b** Label the bays and headlands.
- **c** Shade the rock types.

⑥ **a** Which type of rock forms the headlands?

b Which type of rock forms the bays? Why?

⑦ Think of two reasons why a coast shaped like this is useful to people.

⑧ Add the words *cliff*, *headland*, *bay* and *wave-cut platform* to your word bank and explain what they mean. 📖

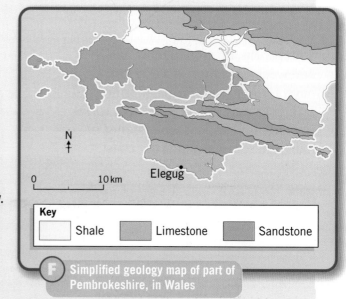

N
↑

Elegug

0   10 km

Key

☐ Shale   ▨ Limestone   ▨ Sandstone

F Simplified geology map of part of Pembrokeshire, in Wales

Features of coastal deposition

Material that has been eroded by the sea is carried along the coast by a process known as **longshore drift** (see **G**).

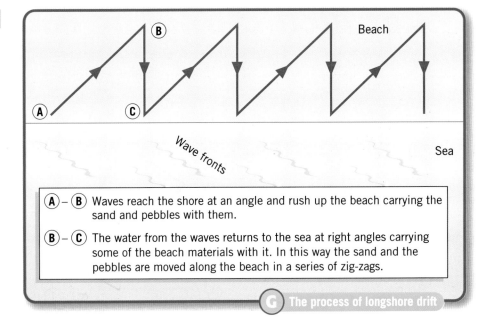

A – B Waves reach the shore at an angle and rush up the beach carrying the sand and pebbles with them.

B – C The water from the waves returns to the sea at right angles carrying some of the beach materials with it. In this way the sand and the pebbles are moved along the beach in a series of zig-zags.

G The process of longshore drift

Eventually, the material carried along the coast by longshore drift has to be dumped somewhere. This is called **deposition**. Deposition often takes place where a river mouth or bay cuts into the coastline and interrupts the longshore drift. Over many years the deposited material is added to and grows out across the river mouth or bay to form a long finger of sand or shingle known as a **spit**. You can see a photograph of a spit in **C** on page 68.

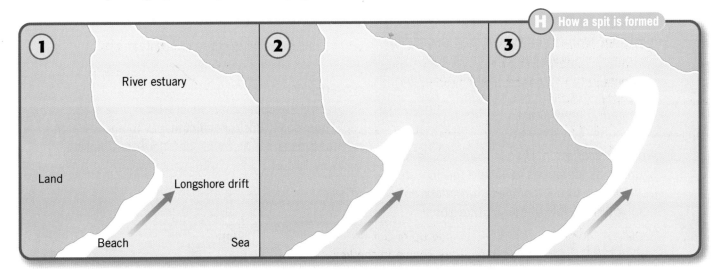

H How a spit is formed

Activity

9 Copy the set of diagrams in **H** which show how a spit develops. Annotate them in the same way as the sketches you drew for the cave, arch and stack. Use the words *longshore drift*, *deposition* and *beach* in your annotations. You could scan your drawings and annotate them using a computer. (ICT)

Conflicts along the coast

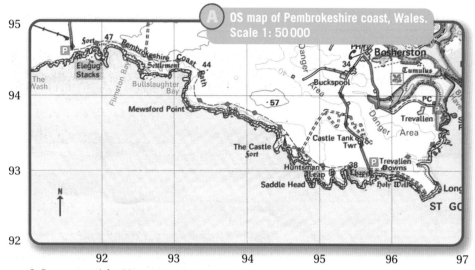

A OS map of Pembrokeshire coast, Wales.
Scale 1:50 000

© Crown copyright. Licence no. 100000 230

Coastal areas are popular for the development of tourism, industry and settlement. But these land uses do not always exist together without affecting one another. There are some which **conflict** with each other. On the area shown on **A** the army shooting range (Danger Area) conflicts with the wishes of tourists to walk along the coastal path.

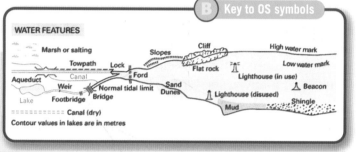

B Key to OS symbols

WATER FEATURES

Marsh or salting
Towpath   Lock   Slopes   Cliff   High water mark
Aqueduct   Canal   Ford   Flat rock   Low water mark
Weir   Normal tidal limit   Sand   Lighthouse (in use)
Lake   Footbridge   Bridge   Dunes   Lighthouse (disused)   Beacon
Mud   Shingle
Canal (dry)
Contour values in lakes are in metres

Activities

1 OS map **A** shows an area of the coast in Pembrokeshire.

a Imagine you are taking a walk along the coastal path. Draw an annotated sketch map of the route you would take, labelling at least four features of erosion and deposition that you have learned about in this unit so far. You could choose from *stack, beach, cliff, wave-cut platform, headland, bay* and *arch*. Elegug Stacks is shown on photograph **E**, page 70.

b Write a description of your route, using six-figure grid references to locate the features. Don't forget to use compass directions to help you describe where you are going.

c Describe what three of the features look like.

2 Look for all the different types of land use along the coast that are shown in the map. Then construct a **conflict matrix** to show which land uses conflict with one another. Explain why two of these conflicts occur.

How to ...

... construct a conflict matrix

Copy the table opposite. Choose six different groups who use the coast and write them in the green user group boxes. Complete the unshaded boxes in the matrix by considering where there is conflict between two users.

- If there is a conflict, put a cross.
- If groups can exist without interfering with one another, put a tick.
- If neither, put zero.

1	2	3	4	5	6
1					
	2				
		3			
			4		
				5	
					6

USER GROUPS

Why do cliffs collapse?

B B C HOMEPAGE | WORLD SERVICE | EDUCATION

B B C NEWS   UPDATED EVERY MINUTE OF EVERY DAY

Front Page 12 January, 1999, 08.00 GMT

World **Beachy Head collapse**
UK **More news soon...**
UK Politics
Business
Sci/Tech
Health
Education
Entertainment
Talking Point
In Depth
Audio Video

B B C SPORT>>

Search BBC News Online

[   ] **GO**

Beachy Head collapse

A huge chunk of the famous cliff at Beachy Head near Eastbourne in Sussex crashed into the sea in a massive landslide over the weekend.

A 200-metre section of cliff loosened by persistent rain crashed onto the beach near the lighthouse.

The rockfall, which can be seen from 5 km out to sea, has been blamed on climate change by some people.

Ray Kent, a spokesman for the Environment Agency, said: 'This was a massive fall, hundreds of thousands of tonnes have fallen away from the cliff face. It has caused very significant damage to Beachy Head. It is basically down to climate change. The level of the sea is rising, so bigger waves are hitting against the cliff base, causing bigger vibrations to reverberate up the cliff.

'This was combined with twelve days of extremely wet weather during the Christmas period. The chalk was absolutely sodden so the combination has caused the rock to fall away. Unfortunately, it could be the shape of things to come.'

Freezing temperatures are believed to have expanded the water which seeped into the chalk, causing it to crumble and sheer off.

Coastguards have warned people to stay away from the edge of the cliff, a notorious suicide spot, as experts try to establish whether further rockfalls could be expected.

© **B B C** ˄˄ Back to top

Activities

1 Study the Internet page reporting the cliff collapse at Beachy Head in Sussex, England.

  a Write out the points that suggest why the event occurred. Underline the reasons in three different colours to show whether it was the weather, the sea or the land which was thought to be to blame.

  b Use your notes to help you write an explanation of why the cliff collapse occurred. Use an *explanation genre* writing frame to help you with your account. 📖

2 Visit the BBC News website or the Environment Agency website to find out about other cliff collapses that are occurring around the coast of the British Isles. Go to www.heinemann.co.uk/hotlinks and enter code 5430P. (ICT)

Case Study
Save our homes!

The tiny settlement of Birling Gap near Beachy Head is teetering on the edge of the cliffs. The English Channel is creeping closer every year, as it has done for thousands of years, eating away at the soft chalk. If nothing is done, the houses will almost certainly slip into the sea in the near future. The residents want sea defences to be put in place to protect the cliff, but English Nature, the Government's wildlife adviser, is against the idea. So is the National Trust, who own three of the cottages. You can read what some people think about the future of Birling Gap in **B**.

A Birling Gap in 1900 and 1999

> There are three houses still lived in and a lovely pub in our hamlet. We want a small wall, or revetment, to be built at the base of the cliff so that the waves will stop undercutting the cliff. The sea defence would NOT detract from the famous view of the Seven Sisters cliffs and the beach would be safer!
> Birling Gap resident

> Birling Gap is a Site of Special Scientific Interest because of the way the land and sea intersect at the shoreline, for its sections of exposed chalk which are very interesting geologically, and for the special habitats and shelters it provides for birdlife and animals. Any attempts to protect the Gap would cause problems further along the coast and probably wouldn't work anyway. They would also spoil the natural appearance of the beach.
> Spokesperson for English Nature

> We own the land and three of the cottages in this area. The National Trust tries to accept and work with natural coastal processes and we realise that we will have to lose land on the coast. We cannot support the building of the revetment and we have offered to buy the three occupied cottages from their private owners.
> Spokesperson for National Trust

> The sea cannot be held back forever. The cottages will eventually fall into the sea because the sea will erode any protection that we put there. However, a small revetment will hold back the sea for the next 15–20 years and would be relatively cheap to build.
> Civil engineer

Activity

1. In groups of three or four, prepare a role play exercise. Each person plays the role of someone in **B** who is involved in the Birling Gap issue and prepares a speech for an Enquiry into the future of the hamlet.

B Some views on the future of Birling Gap

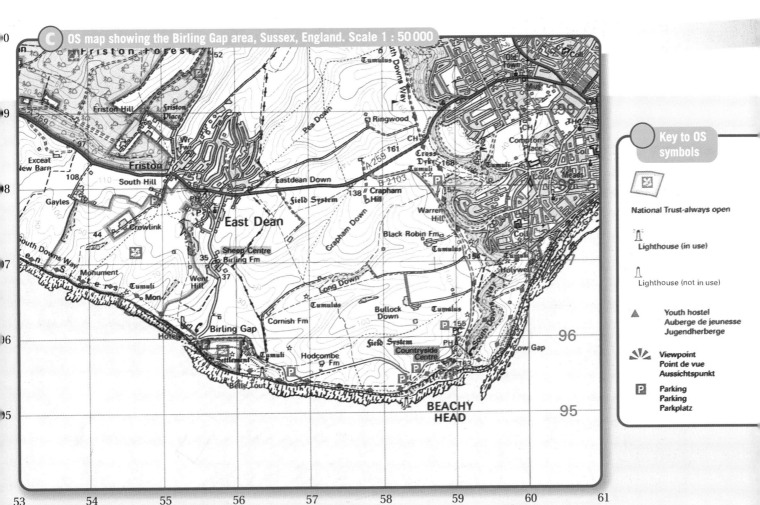

Key to OS symbols

National Trust-always open

Lighthouse (in use)

Lighthouse (not in use)

Youth hostel
Auberge de jeunesse
Jugendherberge

Viewpoint
Point de vue
Aussichtspunkt

Parking
Parking
Parkplatz

© Crown copyright. Licence no. 100000 230

Activity

2 Imagine you are a reporter who is sent to cover the story about Birling Gap falling into the sea. You are going to visit several people to interview them for your Sunday supplement but your secretary has mislaid their addresses. All you have are the notes you made of their names and roughly where they can be found.

a Try to locate the homes of all the people on the table. Write down the six-figure grid reference for each one.

b Discuss how you decided on the chosen locations. What problems did you have, and why?

Alice Richards is just 10 and loves to go down to the beach in the bay when the tide is out. She and her mother take a picnic down from their house perched on top of the cliff.

Bill and Anna Humphreys are proprietors of the Birling Gap Hotel, a large faded Victorian building. Being close to the sea, it attracts visitors from busy cities.

Paul Taylor has spent many years building up his collection of rare breeds of sheep. He is about to buy some more land on Went Hill so that he can graze them more easily.

Melanie Brown lives in a farm not far from the cliffs. She has watched the road to Beachy Head get busier and busier: on a hot Sunday afternoon the car parks along the road to her farm are overflowing.

Mark and Louise Roberts live in the most unusual place on the map. They have just spent thousands and thousands of pounds moving their lighthouse back from the top of the cliffs.

Karen Banks is warden at the Youth Hostel. It is handy for the South Downs Way and only a short walk from the old town.

How can the coast be managed?

It is not only cliffs that have to be protected from the sea. Some lowland areas of the coast are constantly at risk from flooding. It is the job of the local council to protect its residents from the effects of coastal erosion and flooding. They must choose the best way to manage the coast by deciding how much to spend on protection against the sea and deciding what types of protection should be built.

Case Study: Protecting Towyn from the sea

In the winter of 1990 the little town of Towyn on the North Wales coast was flooded when the sea broke through the sea wall. When the flood was over the Council had to decide how to protect the town from future flooding events. They asked for a technical report, and decided to use four types of protection against flooding.

A Flooding in Towyn, Wales, in 1990

B Towyn, North Wales

Technical report

The coastal lowlands at Towyn have been protected by embankments since the eighteenth century. Much of the land around Towyn is only just above sea level, and a sea wall was built to protect the land from the sea.

On 26 February 1990 a deep depression generated very strong winds blowing across North Wales from the Irish Sea. They reached 70–80 knots (140–160 km/hour) at their strongest. Waves were breaking at 2 m above their normal height. The sea broke through the protective wall at about 5 m above sea level and quickly flooded large areas of land.

Very little sediment was carried landward during the flood, because longshore drift had recently removed shingle and sand from in front of the sea wall and embankment.

Activities

Use map **C** and other information from these pages to answer the following questions.

1 Lay a piece of tracing paper over the map. Shade in the area that would have been covered by the floods if the waves were 5 m above sea level when they broke through the old wall. Use the How to ... box to help you.

2 Name four different types of land use that would have been affected by the flood. Give six-figure grid references for the land uses you mention.

3 a How long is the new sea wall?

   b How much would it have cost to build?

   c How much would it have cost to extend the new sea wall to the car park at 988797? (1)(2)(3)

How to ...

... use contour lines to help you estimate

◎ On your tracing, draw in the coastline.

◎ Find the 5 m contour line and trace along that.

◎ Shade in the area inside your lines and use the grid lines to estimate the area that the flood would have covered. Remember: each grid square is one kilometre square.

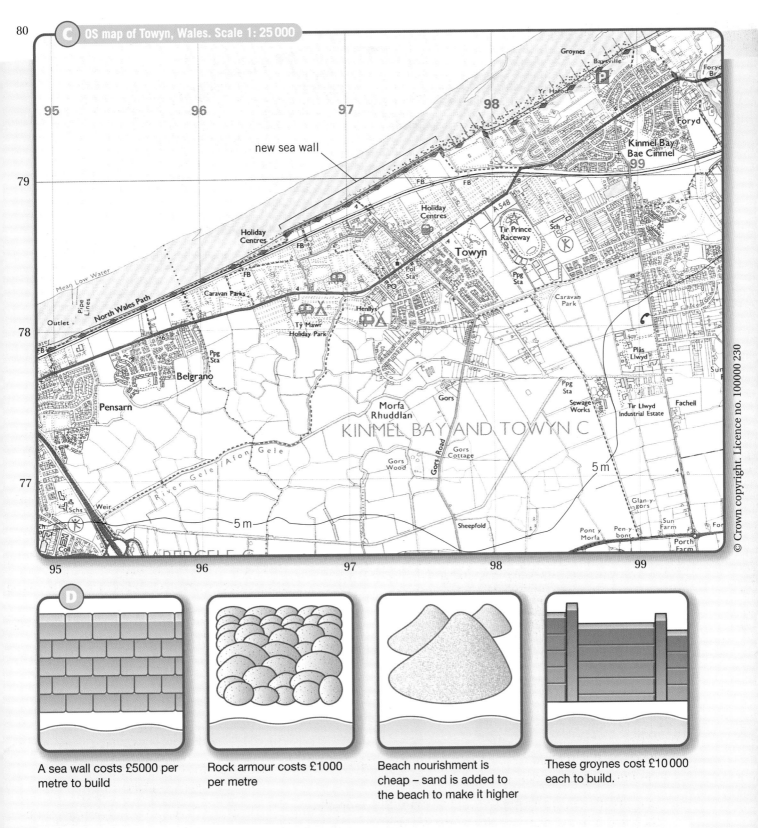

C OS map of Towyn, Wales. Scale 1: 25 000

new sea wall

© Crown copyright. Licence no. 100000 230

D

A sea wall costs £5000 per metre to build

Rock armour costs £1000 per metre

Beach nourishment is cheap – sand is added to the beach to make it higher

These groynes cost £10 000 each to build.

---

4 Rock armour was placed along the front of the new sea wall and ten of the groynes to the north east of the wall were rebuilt. Use a copy of the table to work out how much was spent in all. (123)

Type of defence	Cost
Sea wall	£
Groynes	£
Rock armour	£
Total	£

5 Why do you think the Council was willing to spend this much money on rebuilding the wall?

6 Beach nourishment was also used to protect the northern end of the new wall. Explain why this had to be replaced every year.

7 Why might people living further along the coast to the east be concerned about the rebuilding of the groynes?

77

Case Study

Managing the beaches in Florida, USA

Large stretches of the east coast of Florida have been eroded away over the past century. These losses occurred where beaches were starved of sand because sea defences were built further along the coast to protect the hotels and condominiums (blocks of flats).

Beaches protect coasts because they stop waves reaching the land and eroding it. This part of the Florida coast also suffers from hurricanes. These produce huge destructive waves that remove tonnes and tonnes of sand from the beaches.

Florida spends over US $8.5 million each year on erosion management of its coasts. This is because it relies heavily on the income it receives from the millions of visitors who come to enjoy its white sandy beaches. At Miami Beach every dollar invested each year in beach nourishment returns 700 dollars in income from tourists.

Some conservationists think that protecting the beach with 'hard' engineering (such as groynes and sea walls) is wrong and that the coast should be allowed to erode naturally. This will supply material which will build up the coast in another place. This method of management is called 'managed retreat' and is shown in **C**.

A Sarasota beach in Florida, USA

B A beach in Florida (a) before and (b) after beach nourishment

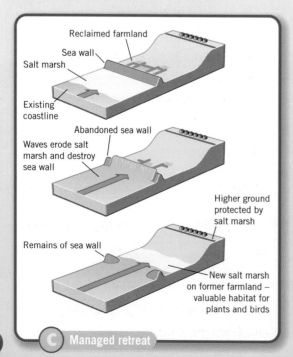

Reclaimed farmland
Sea wall
Salt marsh
Existing coastline

Abandoned sea wall
Waves erode salt marsh and destroy sea wall

Higher ground protected by salt marsh
Remains of sea wall
New salt marsh on former farmland – valuable habitat for plants and birds

C Managed retreat

Activities

1. Estimate how much extra beach has been created in photograph **B**. Give your answer as a percentage.

2. Give three reasons why this part of Florida has been protected by beach nourishment.

3. Do you think that managed retreat is a good way to manage the coast? Give reasons for your answer.

Review and reflect

A Sand and shingle beach in Eastbourne, England

B Chalk cliffs at Selwicks Bay, Humberside, England

Activities

1 Look at the two photographs. For which photograph is each of these statements likely to be true? Try to give a reason for your answer. If you think that the statement is true for both photographs, give a reason for each of them.

a Chemical weathering is occurring.

b Material is being moved along the coast.

c Wave action is eroding the land.

d The council has to keep coastal defences repaired.

e People will bring their swimming costumes and towels when they visit.

f Biological weathering is occurring.

g The land may flood during storms.

h The rocks are more resistant to erosion.

i Caves may form.

j Visitors will come to see the sea views.

2 Write down all the things you have learned to do in this unit. You can find some ideas in the help box – but not all of them are right!

3 Look again at the five geographical questions you asked at the beginning of this unit. Are they the same as any given below? Can you answer them all now?

- What is weathering?
- What is erosion?
- How do waves shape the coast?
- How does the sea erode the coast?
- What features are found around the coast?
- Why do cliffs collapse?
- How can we manage our coasts?

help!

Research

Writing in persuasion genre

Writing in report genre

Writing in explanation genre

Annotating diagrams

Asking geographical questions

Drawing sketch maps

Working with others

Using map contour lines

Using an atlas

5 Weather patterns over Europe

A Satellite image of Europe, 18 July 1999

Learn about

Weather is the condition of the atmosphere. It affects most people's lives every day. Many people need to understand the weather to do their jobs. In this unit you will learn about:

- weather and climate patterns and processes in Europe
- reading weather maps and satellite images
- how to forecast the weather
- the difference between weather and climate
- drawing and reading climate graphs
- how to choose a holiday destination with a climate that suits your family.

What is Europe like?

Activities

1 Maps use words, colours, lines and symbols to show information about places. Look at **B**, which is a **political map** of Europe. There are a number of different types of line on this political map – *coastlines, national (country) boundaries* and *lines of latitude and longitude*. Which of these lines can actually be seen on the surface of the Earth?

2 Use the contents page of an atlas to find a **physical map** of Europe. Now write four lists giving the different types of information that a physical map shows as words, colours, lines and symbols.

3 a Which lines on the physical map can actually be seen on the surface of the Earth?

   b Which lines cannot be seen?

help!

⚙ A **political map** shows countries and their main cities, including the capital.

⚙ A **physical map** shows information about the natural features on the Earth's surface, such as rivers, mountains and oceans.

4 Now look at the satellite image **A** of Europe on the opposite page.

   a What information does this show that can also be seen on political or physical maps?

   b What information is shown that would not appear on an atlas map?

   c Why is this type of information not shown on atlas maps?

5 a Which countries on the satellite image have very little cloud cover?

   b Name any countries that cannot be seen due to cloud cover.

What are clouds and why does it rain?

Clouds are made up of water droplets or ice crystals, depending upon how cold the surrounding air is. These are so small that they 'float' in the **atmosphere**. Clouds form when air cools so that the **water vapour** it holds condenses into water droplets. Clouds are classified by height and shape. There are three main cloud types.

- **Cirrus clouds** are made of ice crystals because they form high up in the atmosphere where temperatures are below freezing point.

- **Stratus clouds** form in a layer or 'sheet' across the sky and tend to be much lower in the atmosphere. They are called fog when they are at ground level.

- **Cumulus clouds** have 'bumpy' tops because of the rising air currents that create them. Sometimes **cumulonimbus clouds** form when air rises very quickly. They tend to be extremely tall.

Some cloud types, such as cirrus, never cause precipitation (rain, hail or snow). Others, like cumulonimbus, bring rain or hail with thunder and lightning. Clouds play an important part in the **hydrological cycle** (**D**).

A Stratus clouds

B Cirrus clouds

C Cumulus clouds

The hydrological cycle

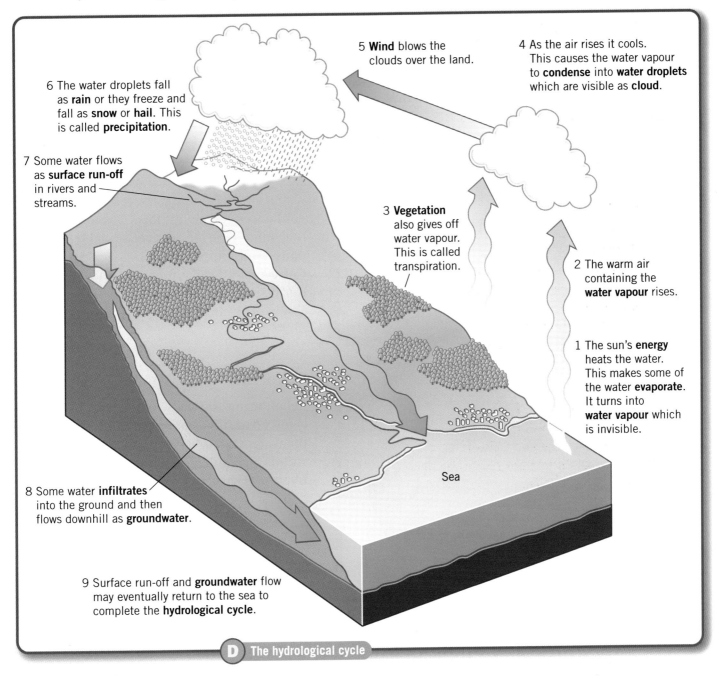

5 **Wind** blows the clouds over the land.

4 As the air rises it cools. This causes the water vapour to **condense** into **water droplets** which are visible as **cloud**.

6 The water droplets fall as **rain** or they freeze and fall as **snow** or **hail**. This is called **precipitation**.

7 Some water flows as **surface run-off** in rivers and streams.

3 **Vegetation** also gives off water vapour. This is called **transpiration**.

2 The warm air containing the **water vapour** rises.

1 The sun's **energy** heats the water. This makes some of the water **evaporate**. It turns into **water vapour** which is invisible.

8 Some water **infiltrates** into the ground and then flows downhill as **groundwater**.

Sea

9 Surface run-off and **groundwater** flow may eventually return to the sea to complete the **hydrological cycle**.

D The hydrological cycle

Activities

1. Start to make your own word bank for all the terms in **bold** print on pages 82 and 83, including those in diagram **D** above.

2. Write a story about a water molecule called H_2O travelling around the hydrological cycle. Try to use most of the geographical vocabulary in your word bank. Use the numbers for each annotation on diagram **D** to help you sequence your story correctly. You could begin your story like this ...

> One day H_2O, a water molecule, was warming himself in the heat of the midday sun when he began to disappear. Suddenly he saw the sea below him and realised he must have <u>evaporated</u> and turned into ...

What causes cloud and rain?

Clouds form when air rises and cools so that the water vapour it holds condenses into droplets. Air can be forced to rise in three different ways to give three types of precipitation: **convectional**, **relief** and **frontal**. It rains when the water droplets become too large and heavy to stay up in the air.

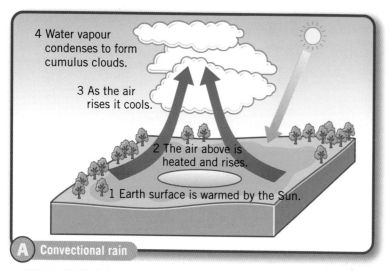

4 Water vapour condenses to form cumulus clouds.

3 As the air rises it cools.

2 The air above is heated and rises.

1 Earth surface is warmed by the Sun.

A Convectional rain

Convectional rain

When the Earth's surface is heated by the Sun, the air above it is also warmed up. The warm air rises but as it rises it cools down. As the air cools the water vapour it holds condenses and clouds form. Eventually it may rain. If the air rises very quickly cumulonimbus storm clouds may form. **Convectional rain** often happens in Europe during hot summer weather.

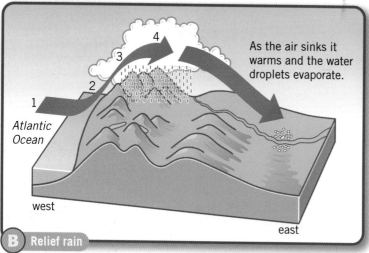

As the air sinks it warms and the water droplets evaporate.

Atlantic Ocean

west

east

B Relief rain

Relief rain

Relief means the shape of the land. When air is forced to rise over mountains it cools and the water vapour it holds condenses to form clouds. Eventually **relief rain** may fall. European weather comes mainly from the Atlantic Ocean and moves towards the east. This means that a lot of the moisture held in the air will fall on the mountains in Western Europe. By the time the air reaches Eastern Europe much of the moisture will already have fallen so there tends to be less rain.

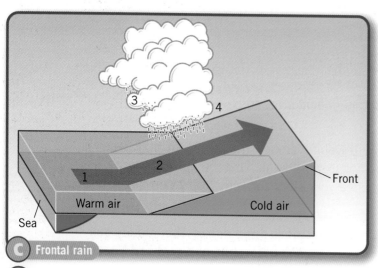

Front

Warm air

Cold air

Sea

C Frontal rain

Frontal rain

Warm air is lighter than cold air. When the two meet, the warmer air rises over the colder, heavier air. As the warm air is forced to rise it cools, so that the water vapour it holds condenses to form clouds. The zone where warm air and cold air meet is called a *front*. On a weather map a cold front looks like this: ▲▲▲ and a warm front like this: ●●● . In Europe, bands of cloud and rain are often found along fronts.

D Satellite image of Europe for 18 July 1999

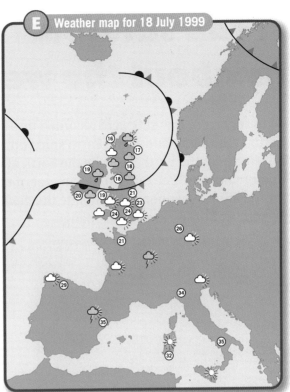

E Weather map for 18 July 1999

Activities

1 Diagram **A** has been labelled to explain how convectional rain forms. Use this to help you to match the sentences below to the numbers on diagram **B** for relief rain.

- As the air rises, it cools and the water vapour it holds condenses to form clouds.
- Air continues to rise until relief rainfall occurs.
- Moist, warm air blows from the Atlantic Ocean.
- The air is forced to rise over the mountains of Western Europe.

2 Use your answers to activity **1** to help you write four labels explaining how frontal rainfall is formed in **C**.

3 Look carefully at satellite image **D** – you can see a larger version on page 80. For each area of cloud labelled **a–e**:

- **a** Describe its location (where it is found).
- **b** Say whether you think it was formed by convection, relief or at a front. Compare the satellite image to the weather map **E** and physical map **F** to help you to decide.

4 Which type of cloud and rainfall (convectional, relief or frontal) tends to affect the largest area of Europe at any one time?

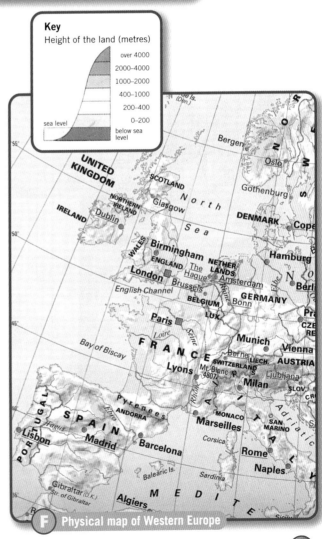

Key
Height of the land (metres)

over 4000	
2000–4000	
1000–2000	
400–1000	
200–400	
sea level	0–200
	below sea level

F Physical map of Western Europe

What can satellite images tell us about the weather?

The images of Europe in **A**, **D** and **G** were recorded by a satellite called METEOSAT. It goes around the Earth at the same rate as the Earth spins on its axis. This means that it stays in the same position relative to the Earth. It orbits the Earth at a height of about 35 000 kilometres above the Equator (almost three times the diameter of the Earth). It can image almost half the Earth from this position. A sequence of satellite images like those on this page can show how weather patterns over Europe move and change.

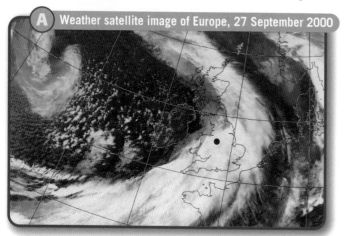

A Weather satellite image of Europe, 27 September 2000

B Weather over Chester, England, 27 September 2000

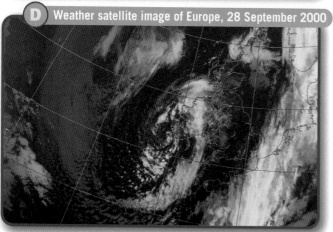

D Weather satellite image of Europe, 28 September 2000

E Weather over Chester, England, 28 September 2000

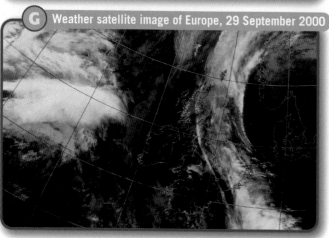

G Weather satellite image of Europe, 29 September 2000

H Weather over Chester, England, 29 September 2000

Key
● Location of Chester

Satellite images provide weather forecasters with essential information. For example, they can be used to track storms and warn people who may be affected by them. Many people, such as workers on oil rigs and in power stations, farmers and ferry operators, rely on satellite images to inform them about the weather.

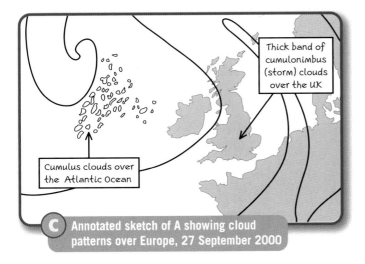

Thick band of cumulonimbus (storm) clouds over the UK

Cumulus clouds over the Atlantic Ocean

C Annotated sketch of A showing cloud patterns over Europe, 27 September 2000

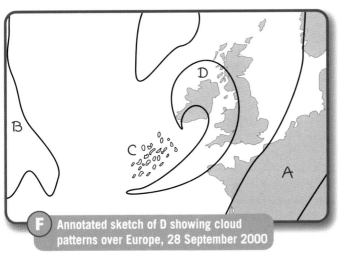

F Annotated sketch of D showing cloud patterns over Europe, 28 September 2000

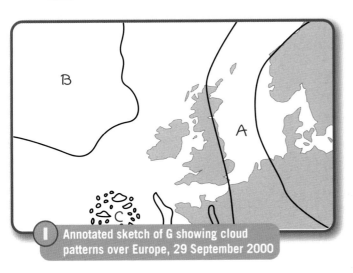

I Annotated sketch of G showing cloud patterns over Europe, 29 September 2000

Activities

Figure **C** is an annotated sketch of satellite image **A**. The annotations describe the cloud patterns and their locations over Europe. Use it as a guide to help you do activities **1** and **2**. You can see the different cloud types on page 82.

1 Match the annotations below to letters **A–D** on sketch **F**.

⑥ Cumulus clouds to the south-west of Ireland.

⑥ Thin stratus cloud over the Atlantic Ocean.

⑥ A band of cumulonimbus cloud over Spain, France and Scandinavia.

⑥ A 'swirl' of thick cloud to the west of the UK and France.

2 Use your answers to activity **1** to write annotations for the areas lettered **A–C** on sketch **I**. Include the location of the cloud.

3 Europe's weather usually comes from one main direction. Look at the sequence of weather patterns shown in images **A**, **D** and **G** and suggest which direction this is.

4 Look at photographs **B**, **E** and **H** and the satellite images recorded at the same times. How do clouds look different when viewed from above and from below?

5 Use the information on page 82 to name the main cloud types in photographs **B**, **E** and **H**.

6 **Extension** (ICT)

a Download satellite images for the last three days from the METEOSAT site. Use www.heinemann.co.uk/hotlinks and enter code 5430P.

b Draw a sequence of dated sketch maps, like **C**, **F** and **I**, showing the weather patterns. Annotate the cloud patterns.

How can weather information be presented?

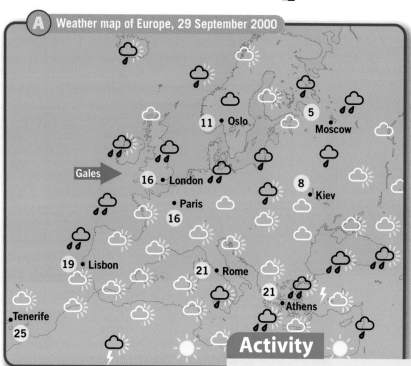

A Weather map of Europe, 29 September 2000

(Labels on map: Oslo 11, Moscow 5, Gales 16, London, 8 Kiev, Paris 16, Lisbon 19, Rome 21, 21 Athens, Tenerife 25)

Meteorologists are people who study and **forecast** the weather. The information they use comes from weather stations, satellite images and computer models.

Map **A** shows the pattern of weather over Europe on 29 September 2000. Satellite image **G** on page 86 shows information for the same day.

Weather stations record a range of different aspects of the weather. Table **B** shows data from a weather station in Chester for the period 20–29 September 2000. Use the Getting Technical box to help you to understand the data shown.

Getting Technical ▼

⑥ **Humidity**: the amount of water vapour held in the air, measured as a percentage. If the air is at 100 per cent humidity, it is likely to form clouds or be foggy.

⑥ **Wind speed**: how fast the air is moving measured in kilometres or miles per hour.

⑥ **Wind direction**: the compass direction *from* which the wind blows.

Activity

① Work in pairs to compare the weather map for 29 September 2000 with the satellite image for the same day on page 86.

 a Write down five types of information which are shown on the map but not on the satellite image.

 b Write down three types of information which are shown on the satellite image but not on the map.

 c How can a sequence of weather maps and satellite images, for a number of days, help people to forecast the weather?

Date	Average temperature (°C)	Precipitation (mm)	Humidity (%)	Wind speed (kmph)	Wind direction
September 20	12	6	89	13	SE
September 21	17	0	78	8	S
September 22	17	0	77	5	S
September 23	18	0	78	6	S
September 24	12	11	89	14	SE
September 25	13	8	86	8	SE
September 26	14	7	88	8	SE
September 27	13	5	86	13	SE
September 28	16	1	81	10	S
September 29	14	2	83	8	SE

B Weather data for Chester for 20–29 September 2000

Geographical enquiry: How do different aspects of the weather affect each other?

Activities

1 Asking geographical questions

It is difficult to answer such a 'big' enquiry question without breaking it down into smaller questions such as: *How does temperature in Chester affect humidity?* Suggest three more smaller questions you can investigate using only the data in table **B**.

2 Gathering information

You can find the data you need to carry out this enquiry in table **B**. If you want to improve your geographical skills, try to gather your own set of weather data and use it to carry out a similar enquiry (see extension activity **6**).

> **ICT idea** Enter the data in table **B** into a computer spreadsheet and then carry out the enquiry.

3 Processing information

A scattergraph is one way of presenting data which shows if there is any correlation (relationship) between two factors. For example, in figure **C** temperature has been plotted on the *X* axis and humidity on the *Y* axis. It shows that there is a **negative correlation** between temperature and humidity, i.e. *as temperature increases, humidity decreases.*

a Plot two more scattergraphs for:

⑥ precipitation and humidity

⑥ wind speed and temperature.

b Why can't you show data for wind direction on a scattergraph?

c Design a way of presenting this information to show whether it affects any other aspects of the weather shown in table **B**.

4 Analysing data to form conclusions

a For each of the graphs you have drawn, say whether it shows a *positive*, *negative* or *no* correlation.

b Write a sentence to describe each one, e.g. *As temperature increases, humidity decreases.*

c Give reasons for the type of correlation shown in each graph.

5 Forecasting the weather

Look back at the sequence of satellite images on page 86 and the weather data in table **B** for the same three days. Use this information and the results of your weather enquiry to complete this weather forecast for 30 September in Chester. Choose the correct word from each pair in *italics*.

> Tomorrow will see the front currently over the Atlantic Ocean moving *west / east* across the British Isles. This will bring *thick cumulus / high cirrus* cloud and heavy showers to the Chester area. There will be a *few / long* sunny spells. As a result the average temperature will *increase / decrease* to around *12°C / 16°C* and the humidity will *increase / decrease* to about 88 per cent. Wind speeds are likely to *increase / decrease* to about 13 km per hour.

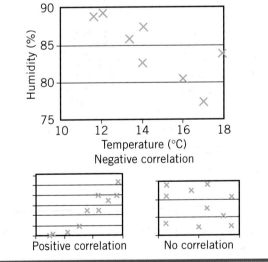

C A scattergraph showing the relationship between temperature and humidity

6 Extension

Use weather data from a school or local weather station, plus weather maps from a local newspaper, to carry out a similar enquiry. You can download recent satellite images from the Internet via www.heinemann.co.uk/hotlinks. Enter code 5430P and follow the links.

What types of climate does Europe have?

So far this unit has focused on the weather. Weather is the short-term or day-to-day state of the atmosphere in a place. Climate, on the other hand, is the average pattern of weather for an area taken over many years (usually 30 years). Europe is large enough to have several different types of climate (see **F** opposite).

Average monthly temperature and precipitation data for a place can be shown on a climate graph like **A**, which shows information for Valencia, Ireland. The red line shows the average temperature, measured in degrees Celsius, for each month – use the left-hand vertical axis to read off the values. The blue bars show the average rainfall or precipitation, measured in millimetres, for each month – read the values off the right-hand vertical axis.

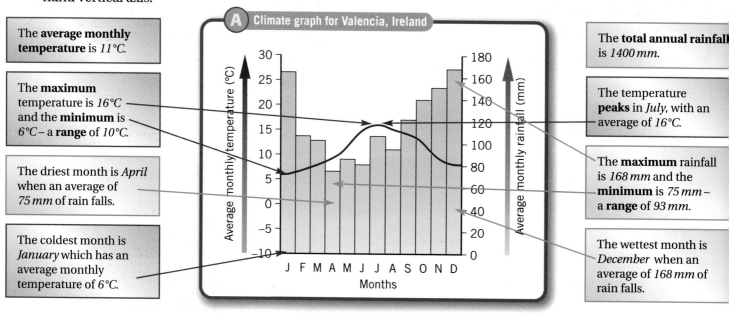

A Climate graph for Valencia, Ireland

The **average monthly temperature** is *11°C*.

The **maximum temperature** is *16°C* and the **minimum** is *6°C* – a **range** of *10°C*.

The driest month is *April* when an average of *75mm* of rain falls.

The coldest month is *January* which has an average monthly temperature of *6°C*.

The **total annual rainfall** is *1400mm*.

The temperature **peaks** in *July*, with an average of *16°C*.

The **maximum** rainfall is *168mm* and the **minimum** is *75mm* – a **range** of *93mm*.

The wettest month is *December* when an average of *168mm* of rain falls.

Getting Technical

- ⓖ Annual – yearly
- ⓖ Total annual rainfall – to calculate this, add up rainfall over all twelve months
- ⓖ Average monthly temperature – to calculate this, add up each monthly temperature and divide by 12 (months)
- ⓖ Maximum – the highest amount
- ⓖ Minimum – the lowest amount
- ⓖ Peak – the highest point in a graph or trend line
- ⓖ Range – the difference between the lowest and the highest amounts

Activities

1. Table **B** shows the climate data for Lisbon in Portugal. Draw a climate graph, using the one in **A** to help you.

	J	F	M	A	M	J	J	A	S	O	N	D
Average monthly temperature (°C)	11	12	14	16	17	20	22	23	21	18	14	12
Average monthly rainfall (mm)	111	76	109	54	44	16	3	4	33	62	93	103

B

2. Annotate your climate graph with boxes of text, using **A** to guide you. In most cases you will only need to change the *data* or the *month* – you can use the same wording. Look at the Getting Technical box if you need help.

3. Shade in the annotation boxes that describe the rainfall in blue, and those that describe the temperature in red.

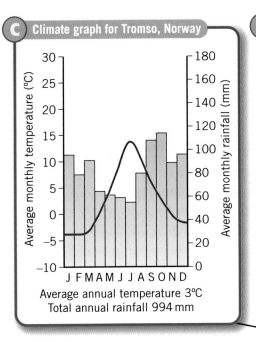

C Climate graph for Tromso, Norway

Average annual temperature 3°C
Total annual rainfall 994 mm

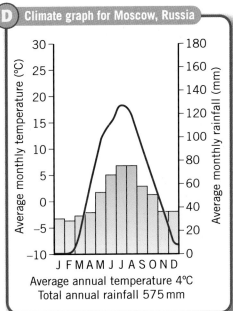

D Climate graph for Moscow, Russia

Average annual temperature 4°C
Total annual rainfall 575 mm

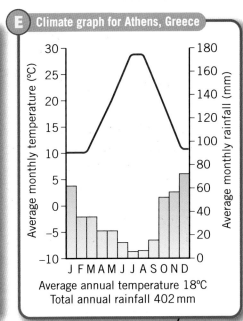

E Climate graph for Athens, Greece

Average annual temperature 18°C
Total annual rainfall 402 mm

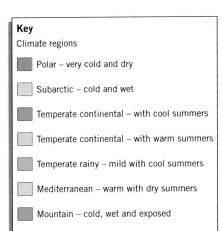

Key

Climate regions

Polar – very cold and dry

Subarctic – cold and wet

Temperate continental – with cool summers

Temperate continental – with warm summers

Temperate rainy – mild with cool summers

Mediterranean – warm with dry summers

Mountain – cold, wet and exposed

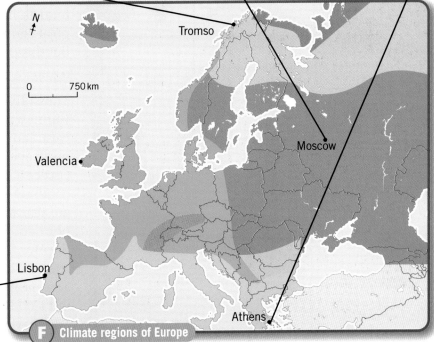

F Climate regions of Europe

Activities

1 For each of the five places marked on **F**, name the climate region in which it is located.

2 a Rank the five places marked on **F** according to their average annual temperatures. Rank them from highest to lowest temperature.

b Do average temperatures generally increase or decrease as you go north in Europe?

3 a Rank the five places from highest to lowest annual rainfall totals.

b Do rainfall totals generally increase or decrease as you go east across Europe?

4 a Calculate the temperature ranges for each of the five places in **F**.

b Rank the five places from highest to lowest temperature ranges.

c Do temperature ranges generally increase or decrease as you go east across Europe?

5 **Extension**

Work in pairs to try to identify any other climate patterns across Europe.

What affects Europe's climate?

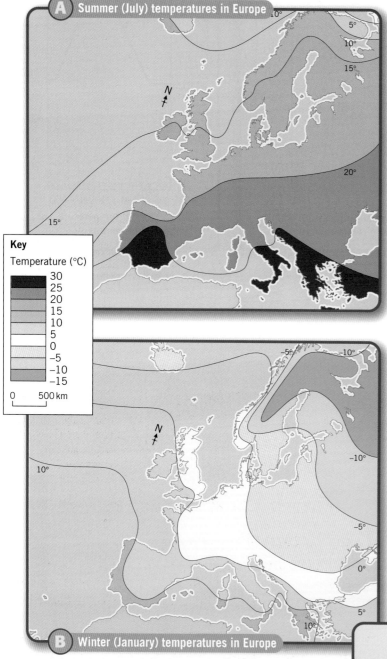

A Summer (July) temperatures in Europe

Key
Temperature (°C)

30
25
20
15
10
5
0
−5
−10
−15

0   500 km

B Winter (January) temperatures in Europe

Temperatures in Europe

Lines on maps which join places with equal temperatures are called **isotherms**.

Summer temperatures

The isotherms for July show that temperatures are highest in southern Europe and that they decrease as you go northwards. This variation across Europe affects many things, such as the types of plants that grow wild or on farms. In southern Europe, where there is a Mediterranean climate, crops such as olives, grapes and citrus fruits can be grown. High temperatures also attract large numbers of tourists. In northern Europe, where there is a polar climate, it is too cold for crops to ripen but sheep and reindeer can be reared.

Winter temperatures

The isotherms for January show that the warmest areas of Europe are in the south and west. Temperatures decrease towards the north and east. In southern Spain, Italy and Greece it is warm enough for farming to continue through the winter. Many tourists are also attracted by the warm weather. In northern Europe and mountainous areas like the Alps and Pyrenees it is cold enough for snow to lie on the ground for many months. This means that farming cannot take place, but it does attract tourists who want to take part in winter sports.

Factors that affect temperature

Altitude

Temperatures decrease by about 1°C for every 100 metres increase in height above sea level. Many parts of the Alps are over 4000 metres above sea level, which means they are about 40°C colder than the coastal area to the south.

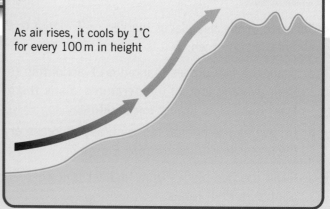

As air rises, it cools by 1°C for every 100 m in height

Latitude

Places near the Equator are warmer than places near the poles. This is due to the angle at which the Sun's rays hit the Earth's curved surface.

In southern Europe the Sun is at a higher angle so that its rays are concentrated on a small area of the Earth's surface. Towards the North Pole the Sun shines on the Earth's curved surface at a lower angle. This means its heat is spread over a larger area so that temperatures are lower.

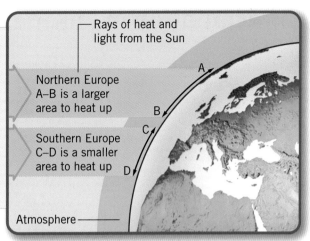

Distance from the sea

Solids heat up much quicker than liquids, so in summer land areas are warmer than the sea. However, solids also cool down quicker than liquids, so in winter the sea tends to be warmer than the land. This means that the distance a place is from the sea affects its temperature:

- in summer, places on coasts are cooler than places inland

- in winter, places on coasts are warmer than places inland.

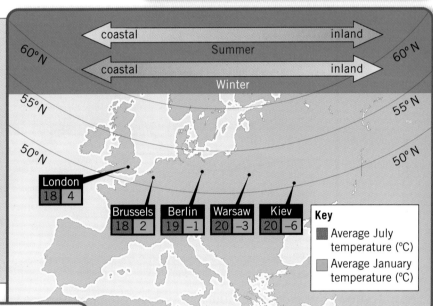

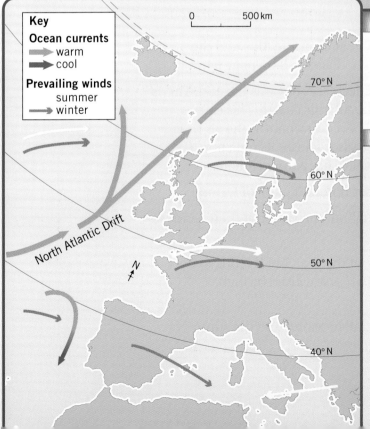

Ocean currents

The North Atlantic Drift is a warm current of water that flows across the Atlantic Ocean from the Gulf of Mexico. It keeps the coasts of western Europe much warmer than areas inland.

Prevailing winds

The prevailing wind is the direction from which the wind blows most often. For most of Europe the prevailing wind is from the south-west. The temperature of a prevailing wind is affected by the area it blows over. Prevailing winds bring:

- warm weather to western Europe when they blow over the warm North Atlantic Drift

- warm weather when they blow over the land in summer or the sea in winter

- cool weather if they blow over the land in winter or the cooler sea areas in summer.

Precipitation in Europe

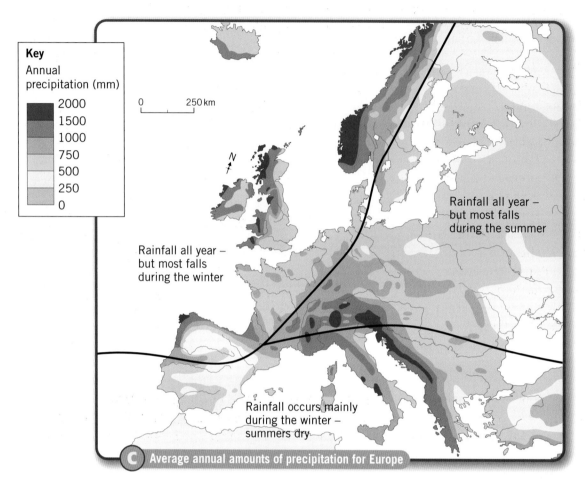

Key

Annual precipitation (mm)

2000
1500
1000
750
500
250
0

0   250 km

N

Rainfall all year – but most falls during the summer

Rainfall all year – but most falls during the winter

Rainfall occurs mainly during the winter – summers dry

C Average annual amounts of precipitation for Europe

Map **C** shows the average annual amounts of precipitation for Europe. It shows two main patterns:

1   Precipitation is higher where there are mountains, such as the Alps and the Apennines in Italy. This is due to *relief rainfall* (see diagram **B** on page 84).

2   Precipitation is generally highest in the west and decreases towards the east. This is because **prevailing winds** bring moist air from the Atlantic Ocean. This causes either *frontal rainfall* (see diagram **C** on page 84) or *relief rainfall* as the air rises from sea level over the land. As the air moves eastwards it loses its moisture as precipitation. This means that eastern Europe usually has a drier climate.

Precipitation falls at different times of the year across different parts of Europe.

🌀 **North-west Europe** receives precipitation throughout the year, but there tends to be more in winter than in summer.

🌀 **Eastern Europe** receives precipitation throughout the year, but it tends to be highest in summer. This is because of *convectional rain* caused by high temperatures (see diagram **A** on page 84).

🌀 **Mediterranean Europe** receives most of its rainfall in winter and the summers are usually dry.

Precipitation and human activities

Some parts of Mediterranean Europe experience **drought** as a result of a lack of precipitation during the summer months. Farmers' crops may die and water supplies for homes and industry are affected. When precipitation does occur, it is often as convectional rainfall. This tends to be heavy and can cause flooding or soil erosion, creating more problems for farmers. However, the dry summers attract tourists who spend a lot of money in some of Europe's poorest countries, such as Greece and Portugal.

In other parts of Europe, precipitation actually attracts tourists. Reliable snowfall in the Alps and Pyrenees brings millions of visitors seeking winter sports. Such precipitation does, however, interfere with farming, communications and industry.

D Soil erosion in Andalucia, Spain

Activities

1 Copy table **E** below, which includes all the places marked on map **F** on page 96. Use the information in the maps on pages 81 (countries), 91 (climate types), 92 (temperatures in July and January) and 94 (rainfall) to complete the table. The information for Zermatt has been filled in for you.

Place	Country	Climate type	Average January temperature	Average July temperature	Average precipitation
Zermatt	Switzerland	mountain	0-5 °C	20-25 °C	1000-1500 mm
Bergen					
Odessa					
Moscow					
Kiruna					
Costa del Sol					

E

2 For each of the descriptions below, work out the place in table **E** that it describes.

   a Most of its precipitation comes in summer as convectional rainfall. Low winter temperatures are caused by the prevailing wind blowing across the cold land surface of Europe.

   b Receives large amounts of relief and frontal rainfall throughout the year. It has mild winters because the prevailing winds blow over the warm North Atlantic Drift.

   c The latitude of this place gives it high summer temperatures, while prevailing winds bring warm air from the Atlantic Ocean in winter.

   d By the time the prevailing winds reach here they have already lost their moisture as frontal and relief rainfall. Its latitude causes it to have high summer temperatures.

   e The latitude of this place accounts for its low temperatures all year round. Its distance from the warming effects of the Atlantic Ocean causes extremely low winter temperatures.

Where shall we go on holiday?

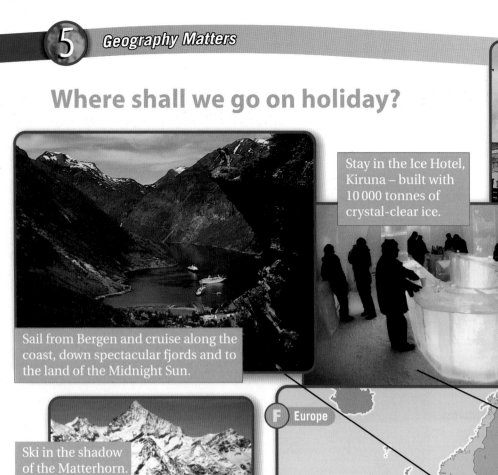

Sail from Bergen and cruise along the coast, down spectacular fjords and to the land of the Midnight Sun.

Stay in the Ice Hotel, Kiruna – built with 10 000 tonnes of crystal-clear ice.

Visit Moscow's famous Red Square and go to see the Bolshoi Ballet.

Ski in the shadow of the Matterhorn. Sample the *après-ski* as you relax by an open fire.

F Europe

Laze on the sandy beaches of Costa del Sol, shop till you drop then club all night long. Any energy left? ... Try paragliding or windsurfing!

The Crimea coastline has many beautiful resorts, splendid palaces and health spas.

Activity

3 Figure **F** shows the locations of the places named in table **E** on page 95, together with a brief description of the type of holiday you could experience there.

a Look back at the climate details for each of the six places and then at **F**. Choose the place where you would most like to go on holiday. At which time of year would you go? Give your reasons why.

b Choose a different holiday location on this page for a family member or a friend. At which time of year should they go? Why?

Review and reflect

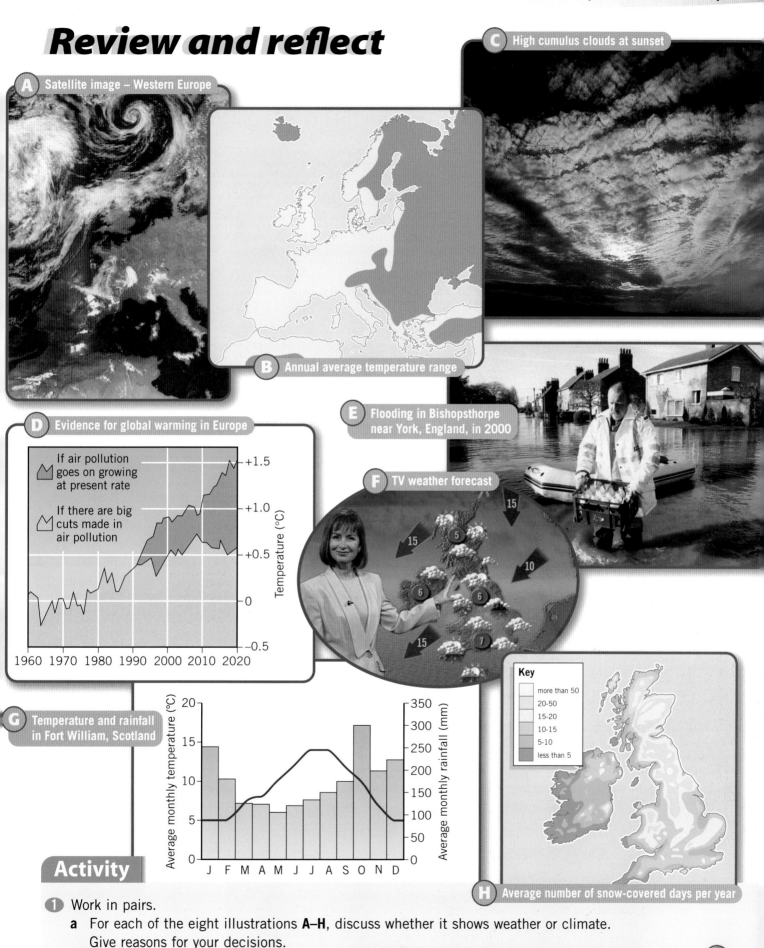

A Satellite image – Western Europe

B Annual average temperature range

C High cumulus clouds at sunset

D Evidence for global warming in Europe

If air pollution goes on growing at present rate

If there are big cuts made in air pollution

Temperature (°C)

+1.5
+1.0
+0.5
0
−0.5

1960 1970 1980 1990 2000 2010 2020

E Flooding in Bishopsthorpe near York, England, in 2000

F TV weather forecast

15 5 15 10 6 6 15 7

G Temperature and rainfall in Fort William, Scotland

Average monthly temperature (°C)
20
15
10
5
0

Average monthly rainfall (mm)
350
300
250
200
150
100
50
0

J F M A M J J A S O N D

H Average number of snow-covered days per year

Key
more than 50
20-50
15-20
10-15
5-10
less than 5

Activity

1 Work in pairs.

   a For each of the eight illustrations **A–H**, discuss whether it shows weather or climate.
      Give reasons for your decisions.

   b Name the type of source shown in each case, e.g. *Source A is a satellite image of Europe.*

Learn about

The rapid increase in the population of Planet Earth is an issue that your generation will have to face. It has great consequences for large numbers of people around the world now. In this unit you will learn about:

- what has happened to the world's population over the past 200 years
- why the population is increasing so rapidly
- what geographers mean by population density
- why some parts of the world are more crowded than others
- what geographers mean by 'settlement'
- the kind of sites which encourage settlements to grow
- the problems that occur when settlements grow very large.

World Population

Planet Earth, population 6 billion

Action needed now to avert disaster

Every day the world will gain another 230 000 people – equal to a city the size of Sunderland. Every week there is another Birmingham, every month another London and every year another Germany to feed, water and clothe.

Ninety-seven per cent of this population growth will take place in the developing world, where most people are already poor.

Good news

Population growth has peaked and is gradually slowing down

Bad news

Growth is not slowing down enough to secure good health for the poor. Their future remains bleak.

Cutting down the growth of the world's population will take time; 40 per cent of today's population are under 15 years of age. The parents of the next generation have already been born.

About 75 million pregnancies each year are unwanted. Between 120 and 150 million women who want to space their pregnancies cannot do so because they have no access to reliable family planning services.

In some ways, reaching 6 billion people is a triumph; it means that people are healthier and are living longer. People are not problems in themselves, but what they consume and how they share the Earth's resources could lead to very great problems that cannot be ignored.

A

Activities

① Use table **B** to draw a graph to show the rise in world population.

② From your graph, estimate the population in 2050 based on similar growth rates.

③ Read the following statements. With a partner, choose the best point on the graph for each one and add it as a label. Be careful – not all the statements are relevant!

- Population reaches 1000 million.
- Growth of population is at its slowest.
- Getting crowded – 6 billion people in the world!
- DANGER! Growth in the numbers of people out of control.
- Phew! Some evidence of population growth slowing down.
- Steady but constant rise in the world's population.

④ Write a paragraph to summarise what the graph tells you about the changes in world population since 1800.

⑤ Read these effects of population growth. Copy out the three that you think are the most important for the future of our planet. Give reasons for each choice.

- There will be more elderly people in the world.
- More people mean more mouths to feed.
- If the world gets too crowded, there will be too little room for everybody.
- More of the world's forests will be chopped down to provide the extra fuel needed.
- There may be not enough clean water for everyone to use.
- If there are more people, it is more likely that someone able to solve all the world's problems will be born.
- There are already over a billion young people aged between 15 and 24 years.

⑥ **Extension**

Look up www.heinemann.co.uk/hotlinks (code 5430P) to find out more about the world's population. Select information to add to your answers to questions **1** to **5**. ICT

The 6 billion milestone

On Tuesday 12 October 1999 the world's population was estimated to have reached 6 billion people. It took until 1804 for the population of our planet to reach 1 billion (that is, 1000 million) people, yet it took only 12 years for the population to increase from 5 billion to 6 billion.

Year	World population (millions)
1800	900
1850	1200
1900	1600
1930	2000
1950	2500
1960	3000
1970	3700
1980	4500
1990	5300
2000	6000

B How the world's population has changed since 1800

Why is the population of the world going up so much?

To understand this, you have to think of the population of a country as a system. Systems have inputs and outputs. If the input is larger than the output, the system will grow. If the output is greater than the input, the system will get smaller (see **A**).

To see why population increases at different rates throughout the world, you are going to look at two very different countries, Mali and the UK. Mali is a less economically developed country (**LEDC**). The UK is a more economically developed country (**MEDC**). Look at table **B**, which shows some basic differences.

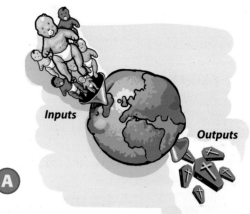

A

Country	UK	Mali
Birth rate	13	50
Death rate	11	20
Annual growth rate	2	30
Infant mortality rate	6	134
Life expectancy (male / female)	74 / 79	44 / 48

B Population facts for UK and Mali

① Copy out table **B**. Work out the figures for the annual growth rate (see Getting Technical) and add them to your table. **123**

② Write a short paragraph to compare the population figures for the UK and Mali.

③ Suggest some extra information which might help you get a clearer picture of each country's population.

④ In pairs, choose one of the 'heads' below. Then choose one of the 'tails'. Write out the head and the tail, and then work out the result that goes with them. The first one has been done for you. Suggest as many heads and tails for each result as you can.

Heads	Tails	Results
High birth rate	High death rate	Population grows fast
Medium birth rate	Medium death rate	Population grows slowly
Low birth rate	Low death rate	Population stable
		Population goes down

High birth rate + Low death rate → Population grows fast

Getting Technical ▼

⑥ **Birth rate**
The **birth rate** of a country is the average number of babies born to every 1000 people each year.

⑥ **Death rate**
The **death rate** of a country is the average number of people who die for every 1000 people each year.

⑥ **Annual growth rate**
Annual growth rate is found by taking away the death rate from the birth rate. It tells you how many extra people there are in a country per thousand each year. If the growth rate is large, the population is growing a lot. If it is a negative number, the population is actually going down each year. A country has a **stable population** when the death rate and birth rate are the same.

⑥ **Infant mortality rate**
Infant mortality rate is a special type of death rate. It is the number of babies who die before their first birthday for every 1000 babies born.

⑥ **Life expectancy**
Life expectancy is the average number of years that a person might expect to live. It gives a clue about the general health of a country's population.

⑥ **Migration**
The population will change if people move either into or out of a country. When people move into a country it is called **immigration**. When people move out of a country it is called **emigration**.

Death rates have been going down all over the world

Death rates generally have been falling in most parts of the world over the past hundred years. There are a number of reasons for this.

Illnesses have been prevented because:

- more people have access to clean water
- more people enjoy a varied **diet**, which means better health
- pre-natal care for pregnant women is improving
- more babies are born in hospital, where expert help is on hand, rather than at home, especially in richer countries
- children are **inoculated** against killer diseases such as polio.

More ill people can be cured because of:

- better health facilities, such as clinics and hospitals
- better knowledge of disease.

Education and changes to our surroundings have helped as well, including:

- better health education
- better living conditions for some people
- more women in LEDCs receiving education
- in MEDCs, improved design for new housing and strict building regulations.

C Clean water helps people to stay healthy

Activities

1. Choose the one **factor** (reason) that you feel has been the most important in bringing down death rates. Discuss this with a partner. Give reasons for your choice.

2. Put the rest of the reasons in order of importance.

3. Start to make a word bank of key words for this unit.

   a Start with the words in **bold** on this page.

   b Add any key words you have learned from pages 98–100.

Birth rates are getting lower but are more difficult to reduce

Photographs **D** and **E** show two families in very different parts of the world. There are many reasons why couples have families of different sizes.

The role of children in MEDCs like the UK

In Britain, feeding, clothing and educating a child has cost its parents an average of over £50 000 by the time it is 17. Children can be seen as an **economic burden** to their parents.

◎ *Schooling is compulsory; careers are specialised*

Nearly all young people go to school, but they cannot work full-time until they are 16. Most adults have a paid job, and some train for years for their career, so couples may not start a family until their late twenties or thirties. When children become adults and have careers of their own, they may move away from the region in which their parents live.

◎ *Old people get pensions*

A well developed system of pensions and benefits means that few old people have to rely upon the income of their children.

◎ *You don't have to get pregnant!*

Family planning is available in MEDCs, so couples can choose if and when to have children. Good health care means that most children are born healthy and survive childhood. Women in the UK have an average of only 1.7 children.

The role of children in LEDCs like Mali

In many communities, children contribute to the family income, so they are an **economic asset**. They often do jobs around the house or on the farm, such as collecting firewood or water. These jobs may take many hours and allow adults to do other tasks.

◎ *Compulsory schooling is less widely available*

Education is often only provided at primary level, especially in the countryside. In Mali, only 31 per cent of children go to primary school.

◎ *Elderly people rely on their children*

Many elderly people rely upon their children to look after them – children are seen as a form of security when there is no state pension.

◎ *Many babies die in their first year*

High infant mortality rates can encourage couples to have lots of children; in Mali, the average family size is 6.7 children.

D A small family in the UK

Marcus and Cynthia Wright live in a small village in Perthshire, Scotland. They both have professional jobs which take up a good deal of time. Marcus is a dentist and Cynthia is a barrister. Cynthia took maternity leave when she was 32 to have her first child, Jamie. Two years later Susie was born. Both parents juggle their time to manage their jobs and get the children to and from school and child-minders, as well as music, swimming and dancing lessons.

Fanta and Samba Coulibali live in Tomora, Mali, with their four children. A nephew also lives with them. They grow millet and struggle to find enough to eat every year. Even if the rains are good, their two small fields only give enough food for six months. This means that the family have to split up during part of the year to find food. Fanta often goes to the River Niger flood plain to help harvest rice. When they run out of food, they have to borrow sacks of millet, on which they have to pay interest.

E A large family in Mali

Activities

1 Read about the roles of children in the UK and Mali. Make a copy of the grid below. Write notes about family size, education, health, children's work and benefits in the two countries. Make sure you include facts and figures.

	UK	Mali
Family size		
Education		
Health		
Children's work		
Benefits		

2 Read about the Wrights. Why do you think they have only two children?

3 Fanta and Samba Coulibali have a much larger family. Suggest reasons why this is so.

4 Use your work for questions **1–3** to write a short summary comparing families in the UK and Mali. First *describe* the main differences, then try to *explain* them.

5 How typical a UK family do you think the Wrights are? How typical are the Coulibalis? Discuss these questions with a partner, then describe what extra information you would need to find the answers.

6 Which of the two families puts more stress on the Earth's resources? Give reasons for your choice.

What age groups make up the population of a country?

This is called the **population structure** of a country. It is usually shown by a **population pyramid**. Population pyramids are drawn with young children at the bottom of the pyramid and old people at the top. In most countries there are fewer old people than children, so the diagrams are usually triangular in shape. You can see population pyramids for Mali and the United Kingdom in **B** and **C**.

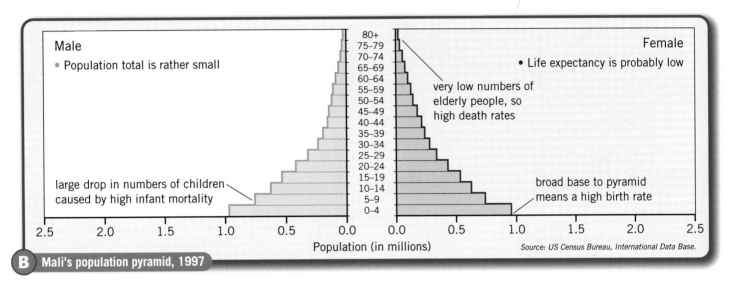

B Mali's population pyramid, 1997

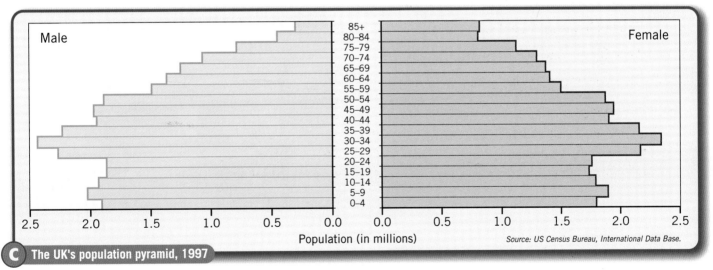

C The UK's population pyramid, 1997

Activity

1. Trace or copy **C**, the population pyramid for UK. Label it in the same way as the pyramid for Mali. You should be able to make these discoveries about a country from its population pyramid:

   ⚅ if many or few babies are born

   ⚅ if most people can expect a long life

   ⚅ the percentage of the population that should be in school

   ⚅ the number of people who need jobs

   ⚅ the number of elderly people, who might need special medical care.

Population density

Population density is a measure of how many people live in an area of land. This is counted in people for each square kilometre (km^2). An area where many people live in a square kilometre has a *high population density*. In cities, population densities can be very high indeed: Hong Kong has a density of over 5000 people per km^2.

A Hong Kong, China, has a high population density

Densities over larger areas, such as a country, are rarely as high as that. Any country with a population density of over 100 people per km^2 is said to have a high population density. The UK has a density of 244 people per km^2.

Areas where few people live per square kilometre have a *low population density* or are described as **sparsely populated**. Mali has a population density of 8 people per km^2. This is a sparsely populated country, even though there is a high rate of population growth.

There are a number of reasons or factors why some areas are more densely populated than others. Look back at the photograph of the Himalayas on page 98. It is not difficult to see why the population is sparse. A city like Rio de Janeiro (see page 124) has a very high population density, and it is easy to see why many people decided to live there.

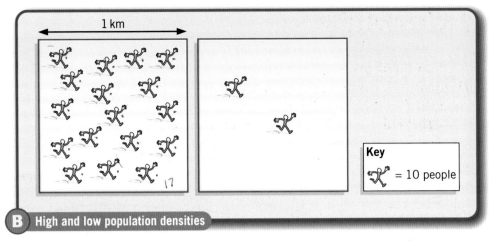

volcanic areas Ḥ

· good roads H

steep slopes L

foggy places L

earthquake zones L

· high areas L

lack of jobs L

· rich soil H

rocky places L

wet areas L

· thickly forested areas L

good farming H

very hot places L

very cold places L

· **temperate** places H

places likely to have blizzards L

places with poor TV reception L

coal-fields H

coastal areas H

river valleys L

dry areas H

difficult communications L

industrial places H

places likely to flood L

sunny places H

cloudy places L

lowland areas H

flat areas H

places with many jobs H

B High and low population densities

Activities

1 **a** Look at the boxes in **B**. Each one represents a square kilometre. Calculate the population density for each one.

b Sketch copies of the boxes. Label them using the key words in bold from the text.

2 Think about the place that you live.

a Does it have a high, medium or low population density?

b List the factors in box **C** that describe where you live.

3 **a** Draw two spider diagrams, one for areas of high population density and one for areas of low density (sparse population). Link up each area with some of the factors from box **C**, as in the example below. Be careful – not all these factors may be relevant!

b Work out which of your labels are to do with people (human factors). Colour code these red. Then work out which of your labels are natural (physical factors). Colour code these green.

c Try to add to your diagrams by thinking of more factors.

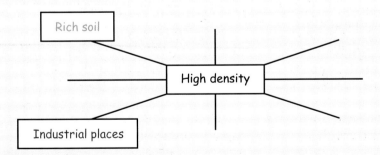

4 **Extension**

🌀 Try to split the physical and human factors on your diagrams into smaller categories (climate, **relief**, soils, vegetation, economic, social, etc.). Use a colour key to indicate these.

🌀 Find the places mentioned on pages 100–106 on a population density map in your atlas. How are high and low density areas shown on the map?

Case Study

Population distribution: where do people live in Mali?

Geographers often ask these questions about the population in a country:

- Where in the country do most people live?

- Why do people live in these areas of high population density?

- Which areas are more sparsely populated? Why?

You have already seen that the population of Mali is increasing very rapidly (page 100). This is because of the high birth rate and the much lower death rate. Today Mali is one of the poorest countries in the world, although it has a proud history – Mali had a thriving and wealthy empire in the fourteenth century.

Much of Mali is in the Sahara desert. The desert has grown since the 1970s, and this has put more stress on the land. Most of the farmland is near the River Niger where the soil is fertile, but mosquitoes breed in swampy areas.

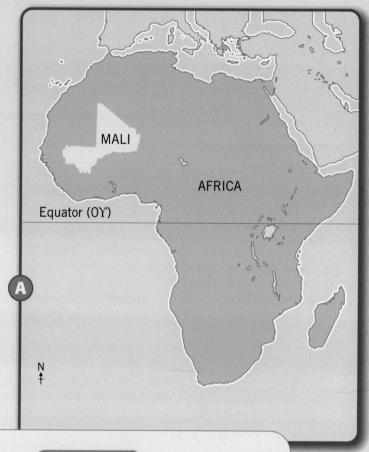

A

Mali fact file

Land

- Land area is 1 240 90 km².

- Sixty-five per cent is desert or semi-desert.

- The land north of 15 °N is true desert.

- In the south the land is over 1000 m above sea level.

People

- Total population is 9.9 million.

- Eighty per cent of the population work in farming or fishing.

- Ten per cent of the population are nomads who follow seasonal rains to find grass for their cattle.

Trade

- Mali is a land-locked country that relies on trade with the outside world.

- Cotton is an important export crop.

- Gold-mining has increased recently and gold could be a valuable export.

Activities

1 Read the information about Mali in the fact file and the text. Photos **C** and **D** may help, too. Make a copy of the table below and add factors (reasons) for a high population density or for a low population density in different parts of the country. Take care – not all the information may be relevant!

Factors affecting population density in Mali

Factors encouraging a high population density	Factors encouraging a low population density

2 Look again at your table. Overall, do you think Mali's population density will be high, medium or low? Explain why you think so.

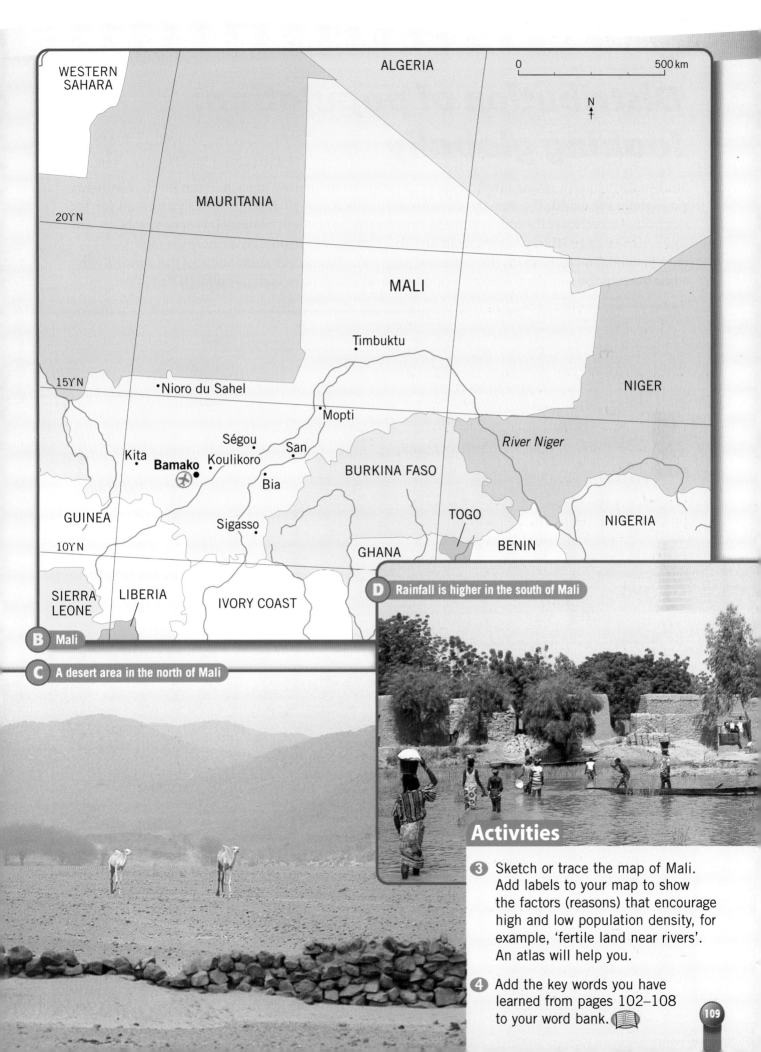

WESTERN SAHARA

0   500 km

N

ALGERIA

MAURITANIA

20ΥN

MALI

Timbuktu

15ΥN

Nioro du Sahel

NIGER

Mopti

Ségou

San

River Niger

Kita

Bamako

Koulikoro

Bia

BURKINA FASO

GUINEA

Sigasso

TOGO

NIGERIA

10ΥN

GHANA

BENIN

SIERRA LEONE

LIBERIA

IVORY COAST

B   Mali

C   A desert area in the north of Mali

D   Rainfall is higher in the south of Mali

Activities

3   Sketch or trace the map of Mali. Add labels to your map to show the factors (reasons) that encourage high and low population density, for example, 'fertile land near rivers'. An atlas will help you.

4   Add the key words you have learned from pages 102–108 to your word bank.

Distribution of population: looking globally

Study map **A** closely, taking time to look at the population density in each of the seven continents throughout the world. The density of some continents is easy to describe and give reasons for. For example, Antarctica is the only continent with no permanent population. It is easy to explain why this is so (see page 107 if you need help on this). The pattern in other continents is more complicated. The pictures on this page and pages 98, 106 and 109 show some of the reasons why some parts of the world are sparsely populated and others have high population densities.

A World population distribution

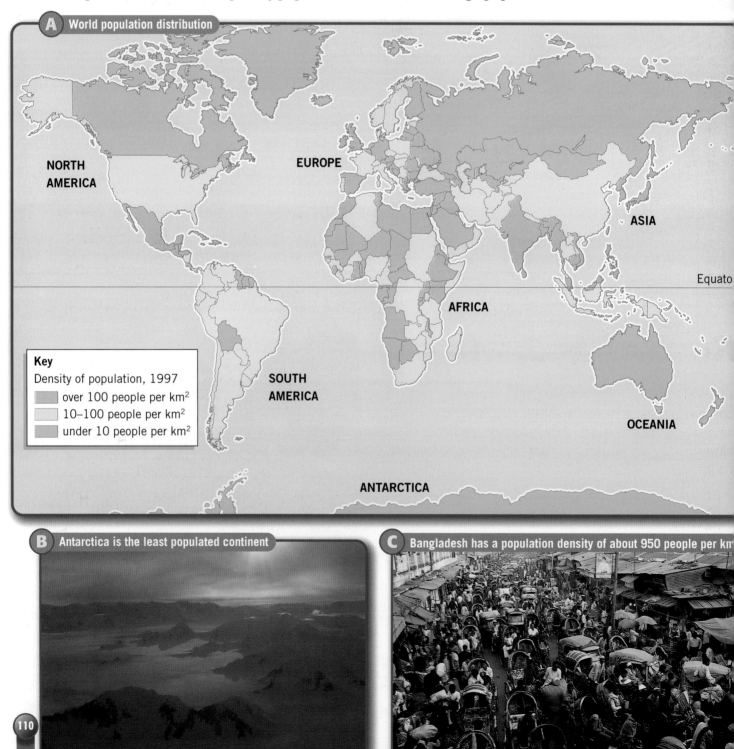

NORTH AMERICA

EUROPE

ASIA

Equato

AFRICA

SOUTH AMERICA

OCEANIA

Key
Density of population, 1997
over 100 people per km²
10–100 people per km²
under 10 people per km²

ANTARCTICA

B Antarctica is the least populated continent

C Bangladesh has a population density of about 950 people per km

Sydney, Australia, has a high population density, although overall Australia has a population of less than 10 people per km²

Fact file

Population record-breakers

- The world's fastest growing countries are Kuwait, Namibia, Afghanistan, Mali and Tanzania.

- The world's slowest growing countries are Belgium, Hungary, Grenada, Germany and Tonga.

- The two countries with the largest populations are China and India.

- Tristan da Cunha and the Pitcairn Islands have the smallest populations.

- Macau has a population density of over 22 000 people per km².

- Greenland has only 0.2 people per km².

E The Nevada desert, in the United States, is sparsely populated

Review and reflect

In this section you have learned about population distribution and growth. Your final assignment for pages 98–110 is to produce a poster summarising what you have learned about population. Use the steps below to help you focus your ideas. Your teacher may ask you to work in a group for this assignment.

▶ Start with an atlas map showing world population distribution. Label the main areas of high population density. Give some reasons for this density. The photographs on this page and on page 110 may help.

▶ Label two or more countries where the population is growing fast, and some countries where it is growing slowly.

▶ Label two countries that have very different population structures. Add sketches of their population pyramids to your poster. Add some labels to explain what the pyramids tell you about the two countries.

▶ Finally, discuss why the world's population is an important issue and some of the ways in which the population crisis could be lessened. Choose three or more ideas from box **F** and explain how each one would help. Add your work to the poster; you may be able to suggest where in the world your solutions would work best.

- Education
- Providing better water
- Conserving the resources of the Earth
- More reliable methods of contraception
- Using less fossil fuel
- Improving opportunities for women
- Tree-planting schemes
- Introducing better types of crops
- **Irrigating** the deserts
- Building into the sea
- Launching people into space to colonise other planets.

F Ways of lessening the population crisis

What is a settlement?

A settlement is a place where people live. Geographers are often interested in how many people live within a particular area (*settlement size* or *type*), the exact location of the settlement (*settlement site*) and what goes on in the settlement (*settlement function*).

You are going to look at the answers to these three enquiry questions:

- What is a settlement?
- Where do people build settlements?
- Why do they choose those places to build settlements?

Where do you live?

Most people, if asked this very basic question, would reply that they lived in a house. Some people might name the place or the road. Most people live in one place throughout the year, and are said to live in a **permanent settlement**. A few people might have difficulty in giving a straightforward answer: they may live in a **temporary settlement** and move from place to place.

Activities

1. For each photograph, decide whether it shows a permanent or a temporary settlement. Give reasons for your choice.

2. Construct a brainstorm diagram. Show as many reasons as you can why people might live in temporary settlements.

3. Colour those reasons why people are *forced* to live in a temporary settlement in red. Use blue to show the reasons why people *choose* to do so.

4. **Extension**
   Research and collect more photographs that show settlements.
   Comment on each photograph in the same way that you did in question **1**.

hint

Be careful, some photographs may not show a settlement at all! There may be no simple answer for some of the others. It all depends upon the reasons you give.

Settlement sites

The exact position that a settlement occupies is often called its **site**.
Many settlements have very useful sites that have encouraged the
settlements to grow. Look at these descriptions of good settlement sites.

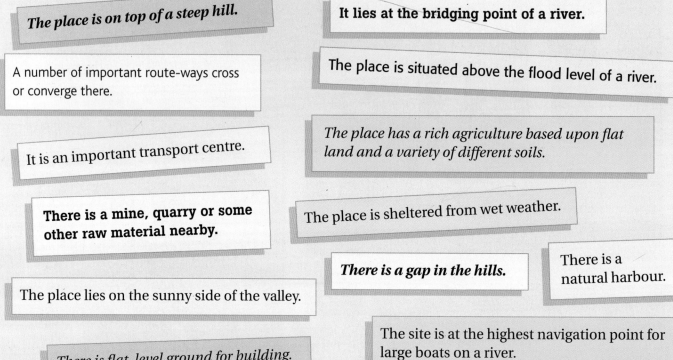

The place is on top of a steep hill.

It lies at the bridging point of a river.

A number of important route-ways cross or converge there.

The place is situated above the flood level of a river.

It is an important transport centre.

The place has a rich agriculture based upon flat land and a variety of different soils.

There is a mine, quarry or some other raw material nearby.

The place is sheltered from wet weather.

There is a gap in the hills.

There is a natural harbour.

The place lies on the sunny side of the valley.

The site is at the highest navigation point for large boats on a river.

There is flat, level ground for building.

There is access to a good supply of water.

The site could be defended easily against attack.

The site of a settlement is not necessarily good; this may mean that
the settlement does not grow as fast as those with more successful
sites. Here are some examples of sites that are not very good.

There is little flat land.

The settlement can't expand because of a major road.

There is flooding from a river or the sea.

The roads have become very congested because they are too narrow.

Important roads no longer pass through the settlement.

The original reason for its existence has now gone.

It's not just a numbers game!

A Extended family group from one of the richest countries in the world

Population is not just about numbers of people. Geographers also ask other questions about a country's population. Some good questions are:

- What age groups make up the population of the country?
- In which parts of the country do most people live?
- How long are people expected to live?
- How many people die each year?
- How many people are born each year?

Governments and planners are also interested in these questions. For example, they need to plan services like schools and colleges, hospitals, houses, shops, offices, factories, roads, transport and recreation.

Activities

1. Choose five of the services that governments need to plan. For each service, work out one or more questions to ask, and your reasons for asking them. Set out your work in a table like the one below. The first service has been started for you.

Service	Key questions	Your reasons
Schools and colleges	What age group do people belong to?	Because planners need to know when to build new schools.

2. Look again at the questions. Which do you think is the most useful? Write the rest in order of importance and give some reasons for your choice.

Settlement along the River Tay

The River Tay begins its course at the village of Kenmore where it flows out of Loch Tay. In fact there are several tributaries which run into the loch, but they have different names (Rivers Fillan, Dochart and Lochay). The river is already quite large by UK standards. It has a typical flow of over 100 cubic metres per second in Kenmore. By the time it reaches Perth, the River Tay has the highest flow of any river in the UK. In fact, more water goes down the Tay than down the Thames and the Severn combined.

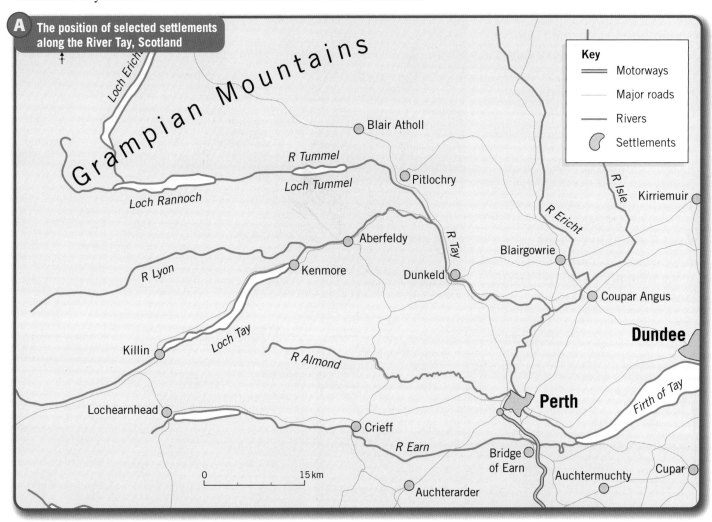

A The position of selected settlements along the River Tay, Scotland

help!

ICT idea

You can find out much more about the River Tay and the settlements on pages 116–120 by entering

www.heinemann.co.uk/hotlinks (code 5430P).

Kenmore

The history of Kenmore village stretches back to the mid-1500s. There has been settlement in the area much longer than this, as you can tell from the many **crannogs** and stone circles in the area. A crannog is an ancient type of dwelling set on timber posts embedded into the loch (lake) floor. Many of these are several thousand years old. But the village itself is relatively new – it was founded in 1540. The original village was actually called Inchadney and was located about 3 km away on a ford crossing of the River Tay. The whole village was moved to its new location when the Castle was built. See this website for more detail: www.heinemann/hotlinks.co.uk (insert code 5430P)

B Aerial view of the village of Kenmore and Loch Tay, Scotland

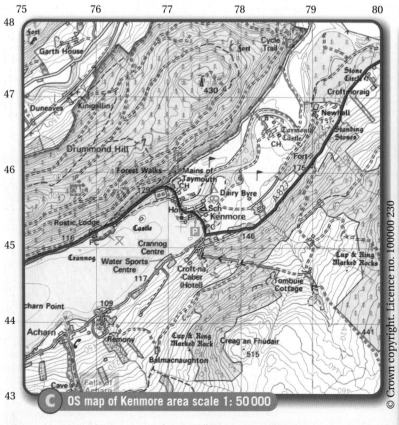

C OS map of Kenmore area scale 1 : 50 000

© Crown copyright. Licence no. 100000 230

D Kenmore – the village

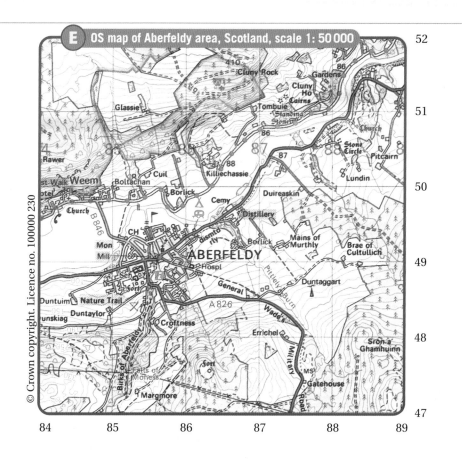

E OS map of Aberfeldy area, Scotland, scale 1:50 000

© Crown copyright. Licence no. 100000 230

Aberfeldy

Aberfeldy is situated at a bend (meander) of the mighty River Tay (Scotland's largest river) and 5 km downstream from Loch Tay. The settlement keeps to the higher ground to the south side of the river to avoid the danger of flooding. In 1733 William Adam designed and built Wade's bridge to carry the road across the Tay.

There are plenty of opportunities for walking around the area. The Falls of Moness and the Birks of Aberfeldy (made famous by Robert Burns) are perhaps the best known beauty spots.

F Wade's bridge, near Aberfeld, on the River Tay

Pitlochry

Pitlochry is the tourist centre of Highland Perthshire. The town is perched between the River Tay and the high hills behind.

The Pitlochry area is famous for its scenery and its hydroelectric dam with salmon ladder. Here the salmon don't actually jump up the ladder but swim through interconnecting pipes. An observation chamber allows visitors to watch the salmon underwater through a large plate-glass window.

The present town is relatively new by Perthshire standards, dating mainly from the mid-nineteenth century. Queen Victoria visited Pitlochry in 1844 and it quickly grew into the tourist town of today.

In common with much of Perthshire, Pitlochry was a centre of flax growing and home-based linen weaving by the end of the eighteenth century. The Blair Atholl whisky distillery in Pitlochry was founded in 1798.

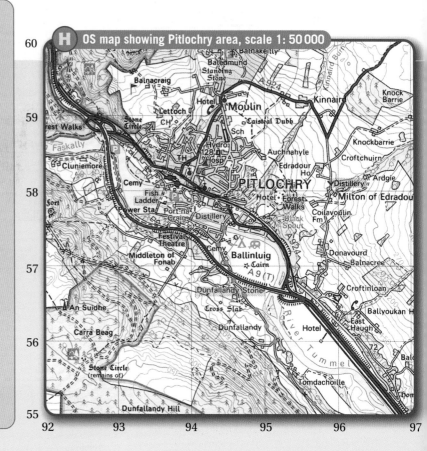
H OS map showing Pitlochry area, scale 1: 50 000

G View of Pitlochry and River Tay, Scotland

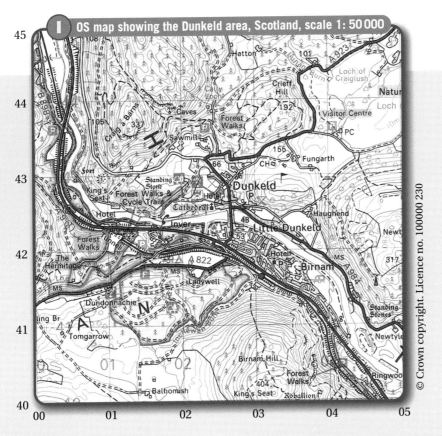

I OS map showing the Dunkeld area, Scotland, scale 1: 50 000

© Crown copyright. Licence no. 100000 230

J Dunkeld Cathedral, near the River Tay

Dunkeld

Dunkeld lies beside the River Tay and is surrounded by wooded hills and crags.

The centre of the village is made up of neat, late seventeenth century houses alongside the ancient cathedral. The oldest part of the mostly ruined cathedral dates from the late thirteenth century, but there has been a monastry here since around 600 AD, founded by either St Columba or St Adamnan.

Pictland and Dalriada merged in 843 AD to become the kingdom of Alba, and Columba's sacred relics were moved from Iona to Dunkeld in 849 AD. Dunkeld became the main religious centre in Scotland. Kenneth I held court here, making Dunkeld his joint capital with Scone.

Perth

Perth was known to the Romans as *Bertha* from the celtic *Aber the*, meaning 'mouth of the Tay'. The city has been a Royal Burgh since the thirteenth century and was a royal residence throughout the middle ages. Perth is often referred to as the 'Ancient Capital of Scotland' for this reason.

Situated mainly on the flatter land on the western bank of the river, Perth is a route centre and bridge point. The M90/A9, the main road to the north of Scotland, passes to the west of the settlement.

K View of Perth

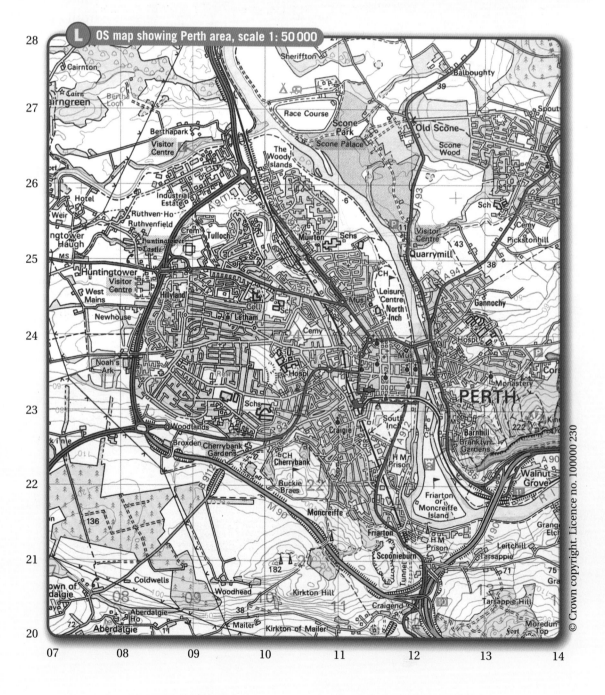

L OS map showing Perth area, scale 1:50 000

Activities

1 Look back at map **A** on page 115 and the other information for the sample settlements on the River Tay. For each settlement, use clues from the maps, photos and text to try to analyse its site. You might like to set your work for each settlement out like this:

Settlement name	Aberfeldy
Settlement type	[city, regional centre, market town, etc.] **Market town**
Location	
Site description	Aberfeldy is sited on the higher ground above the river ... It is a defensive site because ... and ...
Good things about its site	Bridging point of river; main town doesn't flood; ...
Bad things about its site	Little space for expansion except on the flood plain ...
Your verdict	Give the settlement site a mark out of 10.　　5/10
Reasons for your verdict	It is an important bridging point, but defence is no longer important and the town can't expand ...
Special features of the settlement	It could be an important tourist place, because it has a fort, and many opportunities for walking and sightseeing.

2 Use the scale to estimate the size of each settlement you have studied. Find the size of the settlement in kilometres from north to south and west to east.

3 Make a display of your work by organising your notes on each settlement around a large copy of map **A** on page 115.

4 Add words you have learned about settlement to your word bank.

5 **Extension**
Study the 1:50 000 OS map of the area where you live. Analyse the sites of four or five different settlements. How do they compare with those in the Tay Valley?

The living city

In this section, you are going to investigate a much larger settlement. Rio de Janeiro, in South America, is a very large city in a part of the world very different from the Tay Valley. After investigating this city, you should have the skills to enquire into another city anywhere in the world. For any city, try to investigate:

- the location of the city
- what different parts of the city are like
- why there are differences between the different parts of the city
- what changes are taking place within the settlement
- how people are trying to improve the environments in which they live.

Investigating Rio de Janeiro

The first stage in this geographical investigation or **enquiry** is to make sure you understand clearly the location of this settlement. Geographers describe a settlement's location in two ways that are at two different scales.

The site of a settlement means its detailed location, so this is on a small scale. When geographers describe the site, they often look at the physical features of the place it is built on. Descriptions of settlement sites often include:

- details of relief features, like hills and valleys
- the site's access to water, for example rivers or springs
- other details like soil type, vegetation and local climate.

Some of this information might be difficult to find out without fieldwork.

The **situation** of a settlement looks at the broader picture of where a place is located. Geographers often describe the situation of a place by linking its location to that of other places. The situation of a settlement can be described by looking at an atlas.

Activities

1 Use your atlas to locate the city of Rio de Janeiro. Look up the entry in the index of your atlas and write that down exactly.

2 Using the index entry, write a few sentences to describe how it helps you to find where the city is on one of the atlas maps. You could use your own words or set it out like this:

> Rio de Janeiro is at latitude ____ °S and longitude ____ °W. It is found on page ____ of my atlas. It is in the grid square ____. The city is in the country of ____...

help!

Atlas entries are sometimes listed like this:

Wolverhampton	5	D4	52°N	2°W
place or feature	*page*	*grid square*	*latitude*	*longitude*

3 a Use the index entry to find Rio de Janeiro in the atlas. Draw a quick sketch map to show its situation within the continent of South America and the country of Brazil.

b Write two sentences which describe the situation of Rio. Label these onto your sketch map.

4 Look at the picture and the detailed map of Rio de Janeiro. Write a description of the site of the city.

Setting the scene – what is Rio like?

Rio de Janeiro is a very large city of 11 million people. Sometimes said to be the most beautiful and liveliest of all cities, it is famous for its carnival, its samba (a dance) and its natural beauty. It is sited to the west of a magnificent bay, with the dazzling beaches of Ipanema and Copacabana on one side and a forest-covered mountain range on the other.

Rio de Janeiro has two very famous landmarks: the Sugar Loaf Mountain, and a statue called 'Christ the Redeemer'. This statue is sited at the top of Corcovado Mountain, and can be seen for miles around. The map and photographs give some idea what the city is like.

A Rio carnival

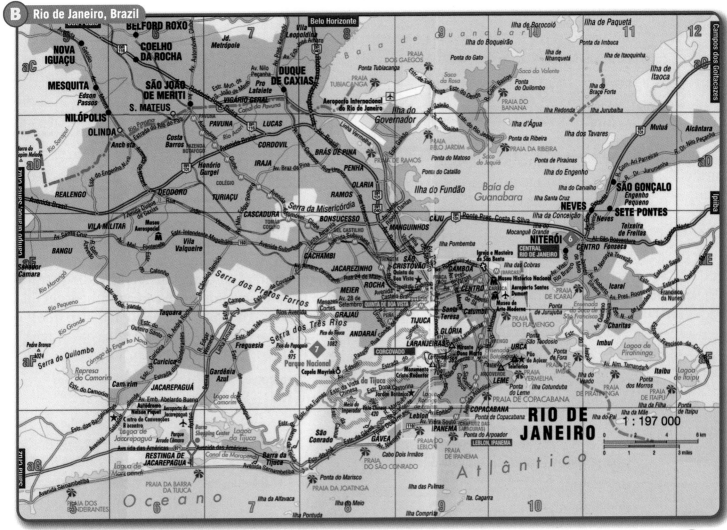

B Rio de Janeiro, Brazil

C Aerial view of Rio de Janeiro, Brazil

 D Downtown Rio de Janeiro

The city centre (or Downtown Rio)

It is difficult to say exactly where the centre of Rio is, because the city is so huge. Slopes and steep mountains rise up so suddenly from the coastline that flat land is in short supply, so the city centre is broken up into many different sections. Tunnels have been cut into the hillsides to connect one part of the city centre with another. The **Central Business District (CBD)** is the area where many shops and offices are located. The old historical centre is also in this part of the city.

The glamorous central part of Rio is busy 24 hours a day. There are busy streets, hectic noise and chaotic traffic. There are expensive shopping areas and constant street trading. Only rich people can afford to live in apartments in this area. Many of the high-rise buildings are part of the financial centre where large firms have their South American and Brazilian headquarters.

Activities

5 Write a detailed paragraph to summarise what the centre of Rio is like. Use drawings, cartoons and maps to make your descriptive work really full.

6 Write a second paragraph about the city centre to explain why this area is like it is. You may be able to suggest what changes you think may occur in this part of the city, and the reasons.

help! ICT

Use ICT to add to your description of the city centre.

- Start by looking at CD-ROM encyclopaedias. Remember to edit text before you use it.

- Extend your investigation by searching the Internet. or follow the links on www.heinemann.co.uk/hotlinks (code 5430P). Use a search engine to make your own enquiry.

Contrasts within the city

It is easy to see the glamour of Rio de Janeiro, especially along the beaches of Copacabana and Ipanema. But there is a darker side to the city. There is great economic hardship for some of the residents. Not far from the beaches you can see serious crime, such as drug-trafficking, and problems in policing. Above all, there is a tremendous strain on the city authorities to provide services for everyone.

You are going to look at three different parts of the city. Many of the poor areas are made up of informal housing or **shanty towns**, called *favelas* in South America.

Rocinha

Rocinha is one of the largest *favelas* in Rio de Janeiro, with about 100 000 people. It is like a big town within the city. Although it is built on steep slopes overlooking Copacabana beach, it is not on the main tourist trail. It is an area of **self-build housing**.

E Rocinha, Brazil

The first residents of this huge *favela* came from the Brazilian countryside 40 years ago to find a better life in the city. A city like Rio thrives on cheap **labour**. Some people work in the factories around Rio's port. Others make a living from offering services around the city, such as selling food, working in bars, cleaning for better-off families, security work or fetching and carrying goods. Many of these jobs are **informal** and may be poorly paid.

When Rocinha was a new settlement, it was made up of wooden shacks. These were often perched unsafely on the steep slopes found all over the city. Now things are different. The houses are mainly built of brick and have rooms with balconies. There are basic services such as electricity, rubbish collection, street-lighting, running water and sewage disposal. Often these services were organised by the residents themselves: they did not wait for the city authorities to act.

Despite the community spirit within the *favelas*, they are still tough places to live. Their crime rates are often unacceptably high. However, by doing well at school, young people can try to escape the poverty of the *favelas*. It is difficult to take a vehicle into Rocinha because of the narrow streets and steep slopes, so its relatively central location is very important to the people.

Barra da Tijuca

The new 'city' of Barra da Tijuca is 10 km west of the edge of Rio. Barra is on the coast, where there is a lagoon of shallow water and flat land, so it has room to expand, unlike Rio which is hemmed in by mountains.

Barra has a population of 150 000. Many people live in high-rise apartments with high security, and there are excellent services, for example shopping malls along the dual carriageways. The beach at Barra is less crowded and more exclusive than those nearer to the city centre. Many of Rio's professional people are leaving the city to live in places on the outskirts like Barra. They can commute back on the motorway to the city centre if they need to, while enjoying the safer, quieter and more exclusive living conditions. Barra has grown very quickly and has been planned in a rather haphazard way. The number of people wanting to escape the chaos of central Rio has put great pressure on this new settlement.

F Barra da Tijuca, Brazil

The area of newest arrivals on the edge of the city

The city's population is not growing any more, but people are still moving into the city. The **out-migration** of middle-class people is balanced by **in-migration** of the very poorest people in Brazil. The causes for this migration are common to many less economically developed countries.

Many poor Brazilians from the countryside struggle to earn a living. They have moved in search of a better life, often to a city or large town. Cities like Rio cannot cope with the im-migration of many very poor people, so these people are forced to fend for themselves. They may occupy land illegally and create *favelas* in places that are not ideal for safe building. The only available space is often the edge of the city, on steeply sloping areas or in areas which may flood (see **G**).

G Favela built on Rio de Janeiro's steep slopes

Activities

7 Use the headings in the help box to describe and explain the three different areas of Rio and its surroundings:

  ⑥ Barra   ⑥ Rocinha (an established *favela*)

  ⑥ The area of the newest arrivals to the city (unimproved *favelas*).

  a *Describe* what each area is like and the kind of lives that people who live there might lead.

  b *Explain* why the area is like it is and how it might change in the future.

help!

Include information about the location, the physical geography of the area, the jobs people do, the type of housing, and the services offered. Add detail by searching the Internet, as you did for the city centre. **ICT**

Activities

8 Your final task is to produce a labelled poster to summarise the contrasts in the city of Rio. You may be asked to work in a pair or a group for this activity.

   a Draw a sketch map of the city. Label the city centre, Rocinha, Barra da Tijuca and the latest developments on the outskirts of Rio.

   b Present the most important parts from your answers to **5**, **6** and **7** as bullet points. Try to show the main changes in each area. Remember that the poster is about *contrasts* within the city. Include illustrations from a number of sources.

9 **Extension**
Make a presentation to show how the parts of your poster are linked to each other. It may help to use another colour for this. Think about the movement of people throughout the city every day, as well as long-term migrations, and about different types of jobs in the city, for example formal and informal work.

Review and reflect

Summary of the Rio de Janeiro investigation

	Page
Geographers often start their investigations into places by locating them. You found out the **situation** of Rio by using an atlas.	122
More detailed maps and photographs of the city showed you the **site** of the settlement, the place where it is built.	123–124
Like many towns and cities, Rio has a central area which geographers call the **central business district**.	124
Outside the centre of the city, there are great contrasts between different neighbourhoods. In cities like Rio the pressure for housing is often so great that people are forced to build their own houses.	125–126

In time, some areas of self-build housing, or ***favelas***, are improved. But on the edge of the city, new arrivals have to find a home.

Activities

In this section you have learned about contrasting settlements.

Look back at your work on Rio de Janeiro using the page numbers in the summary table above to help.

1 In pairs, test that you understand what the key words (in bold) mean. For each word, try to think of another place where you can describe an example.

2 Discuss what was the most interesting thing you found out, a new skill you learned and something you need to improve upon.

Flood disaster

How do people cope?

How do people cope?

Learn about

Damage from flooding across the world is greater than from any other form of natural disaster. Understanding the causes and effects of floods can help people to manage the problems that they create. In this unit you will learn:

- what happens to water when it lands on the ground
- what causes floods
- how people respond to floods
- how the effects of flooding in the United Kingdom are different from those in Mozambique.

A

In February 2000, Mozambique, a country in south-east Africa, suffered devastating flooding. Look carefully at photograph **A** on the opposite page. The dry land around the base of the tree is keeping a family safe from the flooded rivers.

Activities

1 Work in pairs to answer the following questions.

   a Who do you think took this photograph?

   b What might the view from the top of the tree look like?

   c How many people are on the dry land in the photograph?

   d How big do you think the piece of dry land is?

   e Name five things, other than people, that are on the dry land.

   f Why do you think these things were important enough for the family to save?

   g Name three things in the tree.

   h Why do you think they have put these things in the tree?

   i What other things, that cannot be seen, will the family need to survive?

   j Where will they go to the toilet?

   k Why might this cause problems?

   l Is the weather warm or cold?

   m What is the evidence for this?

   n What shelter does the family have?

   o Why might this be a problem?

   p Why might these people be waiting, rather than trying to escape?

   q Who might rescue them, and how?

2 Do you think Mozambique is a rich or a poor country?

3 What impact will this have on how Mozambique copes with flooding?

In 1998 large areas of the United Kingdom were affected by flooding. Over the Easter holiday, flooding caused damage worth £400 million, five people died and more than 1500 people were **evacuated** from their homes. Then, in October 1998, about 8000 square kilometres of England and Wales were flooded. The River Wye was 5 metres above its winter level and more than 160 kilometres of the River Severn were on red flood warning alert. Two thousand homes were cut off by flood water for two days.

Activities

4 Using the questions in activity **1** above to help you, write down five geographical questions you could ask someone about photograph **B**. Your questions should try to make that person think carefully about how flooding affects people's lives, and how the people might feel about it.

5 Swap questions with another person. Answer each other's questions.

6 In a pair, compare your questions and decide on the best five. Write down what you think makes a good geographical question.

7 The United Kingdom is a much richer country than Mozambique. How will this affect the ways in which it copes with flooding?

Understanding flooding: what happens to water when it reaches the ground?

Water lands on the Earth's surface as **precipitation**. Precipitation is part of a never-ending process called the **water cycle**. The simplified version of the water cycle in figure **A** shows how water **evaporates** from the sea and land, rises and **condenses** to form clouds. It then falls back to Earth as precipitation. To understand how flooding is caused it is important to know what happens to water when it reaches the ground. When precipitation lands on the Earth's surface it will either:

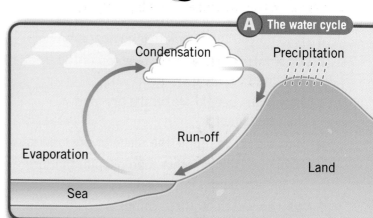

A The water cycle

- ◎ **infiltrate** (sink in) and flow as **groundwater** into rivers or be used and **transpired** by plants

- ◎ lie on the ground surface and eventually **evaporate**

- ◎ flow over the surface of the ground as **surface run-off**.

Whether or not the water infiltrates depends on many different factors, such as:

- ◎ if the ground is **permeable** or **impermeable**

- ◎ if the ground is flat or sloping

- ◎ how heavily the rain is falling.

Water which flows over the land as surface run-off tends to reach rivers much more quickly than groundwater.

Getting Technical ▼

Precipitation

Water falling from the air to Earth as rain, hail, sleet or snow.

Evaporation

The change of water from a liquid, which is visible, to water vapour, which is an invisible gas.

Transpiration

Water vapour given off by plants into the air.

Condensation

The change of invisible water vapour in the air into liquid droplets which are visible as cloud.

Surface run-off

The flow of water over the ground surface, including rivers and streams.

Groundwater flow

The flow of water beneath the ground surface. The water has to seep between the air spaces in soil and rocks, which makes it slower than surface run-off.

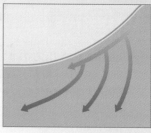

Infiltration

When water sinks into the ground.

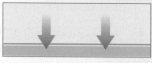

Permeable

Ground that allows water to pass through it.

Impermeable

Ground that does not allow water to pass through it.

Activities

Fieldwork enquiry
Asking questions

You are going to investigate one big enquiry question:

> **What happens to water when it reaches the ground?**

1 You must answer some geographical questions by carrying out a piece of fieldwork in your school grounds.

What happens to water when:

a it lands on a flat surface?

b it lands on a sloping surface?

c it lands on a permeable surface such as grass or soil?

d it lands on an impermeable surface such as concrete or tarmac?

e it falls quickly or heavily?

f it falls slowly or gently?

2 Gathering information

a Go out into your school grounds with a watering-can full of water and carry out research into questions **1a–f** above. Observe the water landing on different types of surface at different rates (heavily and gently). Record exactly what happens each time using words from the Getting Technical box.

b When you get back to the classroom, write the title:

What happens to water when it reaches the ground?

Then write the side-heading *Method* and describe exactly what you did in order to research the enquiry questions.

3 Processing your information

a Design a table to show your results. Include drawings that show clearly what happened at each place where you poured the water.

b Find a way to show the results on a map of your school.

4 Describing and explaining your results

Write the side-heading *Conclusions*. For each of the six questions **1a–f** above, describe what happened and give as many reasons for this as you can. You *must* use the following words in your answers:

**infiltrate   permeable   impermeable
surface run-off**

5 Predict what will happen to water when:

a it lands on steeply sloping permeable ground

b it falls very gently onto flat impermeable ground

c it falls quickly onto flat permeable ground.

6 Suggest three more geographical questions about 'What happens to water when it reaches the ground?' that you could have investigated.

7 How does knowing about what happens to water when it reaches the ground help people to understand why rivers flood? Try to include something about *infiltration, permeable* and *impermeable ground, surface run-off, groundwater flow* and *transpiration*.

What causes the River Tay in Scotland to flood?

A The River Tay, Scotland, flooding around Perth in January 1993

The River Tay is 188 km long and is Scotland's longest river. It rises in the Scottish highlands and flows swiftly eastwards to the Firth of Tay at Perth. The town of Perth is built on the banks of the River Tay and is a major bridging point along the river. The map on page 115 shows the location of Perth.

In the middle of January 1993 the River Tay flooded parts of Perth and the surrounding areas. A river flood happens when there is too much water for the river channel to hold. This causes the water in the channel to overflow and cover the nearby land. The River Tay often floods, but this flood was the worst in 150 years. River flooding along the Tay is caused by a combination of physical and human factors.

Factors that cause the River Tay to flood

The amount of precipitation

The area of Scotland where the River Tay has its source has a large amount of precipitation. This means that there is a lot of water to drain away in rivers. On Saturday 16 January 1993 a storm with winds of up to 240 kph combined with torrential rain and the continuing snow thaw meant that the land was unable to absorb any more moisture.

The size of the drainage basin

The area of land drained by a river is called its **drainage basin**. The River Tay's drainage basin is 9600 km² – the largest in Scotland. This means it has to drain away more precipitation than smaller basins.

The steepness of the slopes

The River Tay begins its journey to the North Sea in the Grampian Mountains. Much of the land here is very steep, so precipitation flows quickly into the river.

The type of vegetation

Most of the River Tay's drainage basin is covered by moorland and grassland. This type of **vegetation** does not use up and transpire as much water as trees. Although the basin was once covered in woodland, people have cut down most of the trees to make space for farming.

The number of tributaries

The higher the number and the greater the size of the **tributaries** in a drainage basin, the quicker the water will reach the main river. The River Tay has many large tributaries, including Rivers Almond, Earn, Ericht, Isla and Tummel. This increases the risk of flooding downstream from them. By the time it reaches Perth, the River Tay has the highest flow of any river in the UK. In fact, more water goes down the Tay than down the Thames and the Severn combined.

Building towns and cities

The River Tay has many villages and towns along its course, such as Perth, Bridge of Earn, Dunkeld, Aberfeldy and Pitlochry (see map **A** on page 115). In these built-up areas, impermeable surfaces increase the risk of flooding because they cause surface run-off, which reaches the river quickly. Impermeable surfaces can also stop floodwater from infiltrating so that the flooding lasts longer.

B Front gardens, after River Tay, Perth, Scotland, flooded

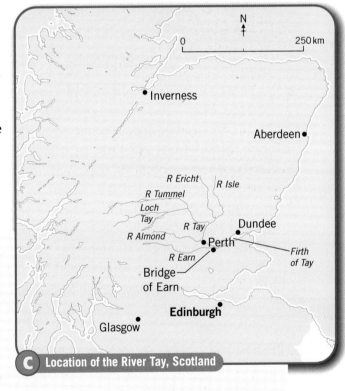

C Location of the River Tay, Scotland

Activities

1. What is a river flood?

2. Copy the table below. Write each of the physical and human causes of flooding for the River Tay into the correct column.

Physical causes	Human causes

3. Name the five main tributaries of the River Tay.

4. Using map **A** on page 115, which tributary joins the River Tay to the south of Perth?

5. Look at photograph **B** and map **C**. Can you suggest reasons why Bridge of Earn was so badly hit by the floods?

6. Explain why in towns the water level took many days to lower.

7. Study photographs **A** and **B**. How do you think people living in this area will be affected by floods? Make five suggestions.

What are the effects of the River Tay flooding?

Activities

Getting to know the area on the map

1 The River Tay flows from north to south on map **B**. Follow the course of the river with your finger from where it appears on the map to where it leaves the map.

   a Is the name of the last part of Perth you pass Muirton or Friarton?

   b How many road bridges cross the River Tay on the map?

   c What other type of bridge crosses the River Tay?

2 Look carefully at the uses of the land next to the River Tay as it flows through Perth.

   a Make a list of the uses of the land along the River Tay.

   b What is the most common use of the land along the river?

   c Why do you think the land has not been greatly used for buildings?

Flooding at North Muirton, January 1993

3 **a** *Friday 15 January: Storm warnings issued by the Met office.*

   b *Saturday 16 January: Torrential rain and melting snows increase water levels in the upper course of the River Tay. SEPA issues a flood warning.* What do the letters SEPA stand for (see **A**)?

   c *Sunday 17 January: SEPA puts Perth on a severe flood warning alert.* What is a 'severe flood warning'?

   d *Monday 18 January: The River Tay has flooded many parts of Perth.*

     i Give the six-figure grid references for the following badly affected areas: Muirton and North Inch.

    ii *The golf course at North Inch was under 2 m of water.* Give the six-figure grid reference of the golf course clubhouse.

   iii *Residents had to be rescued from their homes by inflatable boats and taken to safety in local schools.* Which school would be the safest, the one at 110252 or the one at 102244? Give reasons for your choice.

   iv The rising water blocked roads through the centre of Perth, grid square 1123. Look carefully at map **B**. Work out a safe route for the emergency services to reach Muirton from the south of Perth.

Floodline
0845 988 1188
Scottish Environment
Protection Agency

All Clear

Flood
Watch

Flood
Warning

Means flooding of homes and
main roads is expected. Act now!

Severe
Flood
Warning

Means serious flooding is expected.
There is imminent danger to life and property.
Act now!

A Flood protection poster

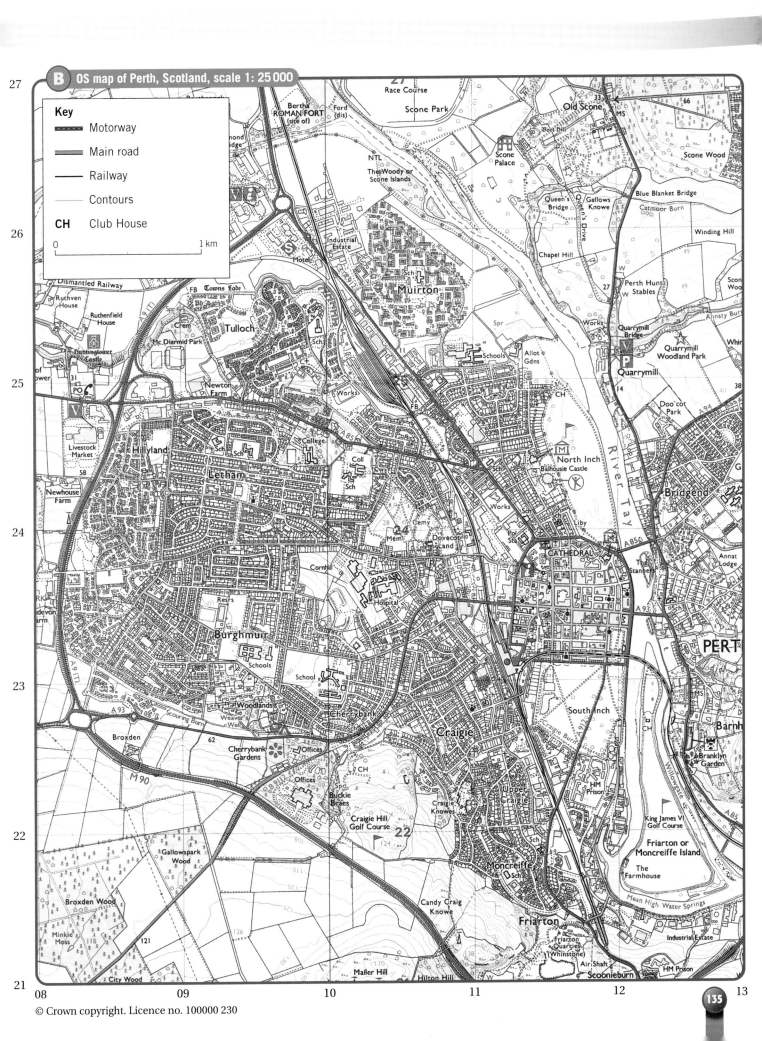

Key
Motorway
Main road
Railway
Contours
CH   Club House

0   1 km

How do people respond to floods in the United Kingdom?

Activities

1 Use a long ruler to measure a depth of 60 cm. Imagine that your home gets flooded with water this deep.

a Make a list of all the damage and problems that might be caused by the water, both inside and outside your home.

b If the flooding in your local area lasts for a week, what further problems might be created for you and the rest of your family? Add these to your list.

c List all the things your family could have done, or could do, to reduce the damage and problems caused by the flood.

d List other people or organisations that might have been able to help, and say what sort of help each one could have provided.

e Work together in groups of three or four. Classify the people and organisations you have listed for **d** into three to six categories by grouping them together. For example, you might group the police, fire and ambulance services together.

f Agree on a 'heading' for each category, for example 'Emergency Services'. Design a way to record your group's classified ideas clearly.

2 a Read the story of Fiona and Mark Dodd and the 1998 floods.

b Draw a table with three columns with the headings *before*, *during* and *after*. Write in what the Dodds did and felt during and after the flood. Write in the names of the people and organisations that could have provided help before, during and after the flood.

3 Imagine that you are the Mayor of Northampton. You have been asked to write the Council's Flood Plan. The aim of the plan is to stop or reduce flood problems in the future. It must include three sections:

- stopping floods or flood damage from happening
- warning people when a flood may happen
- responding to the emergency when a flood has happened.

Use your information about organisations and people who can help *before*, *during* and *after* a flood in your plan.

A Firefighters organising a rescue in flooded Leamington Spa, England, 1998

Fiona and Mark Dodd and the 1998 floods

In the weeks before Easter 1998 it rained very heavily across England and Wales.
On *Thursday 9 April*, one month's rain had fallen in 24 hours, and heavy rain was forecast for most of Friday and Saturday in the Midlands.

Fiona and Mark Dodd live with their two young children in Far Cotton near Northampton, close to the River Nene. Just after *midnight*, early on *Friday 10 April*, a policeman called to say that the Environment Agency had put out a flood warning. Half an hour later polluted water swept through the houses in their village. Within minutes the water was 30 cm deep so Mark took the children upstairs. Fiona tried to keep the rising water out with a bucket and pans ... but it was hopeless. They rang Mark's brother, who lives 3 miles away, but he couldn't drive beyond the end of his flooded street.

At *2.00 a.m.* the flood water cut off the power supply. The Dodds tried to move their most valuable possessions upstairs in the dark but in the panic their wedding photographs and earliest pictures of their children were lost. 'How can I tell my daughter as she grows up that I have no photographs of her as a baby?' Fiona cried to a BBC news reporter the following day. 'Our furniture, carpets, washing-machine, television ... everything downstairs is ruined. Our sense of security has been shattered in a terrifying seven hours of cold, wet, pitch-blackness.' Mrs Scott, an elderly neighbour, was filmed as she was carried out of her house by paramedics. She was suffering from hypothermia.

Northamptonshire County Council arranged for flood victims to move into the primary school hall in the next village for the *Easter weekend*. Social Services provided the Dodds and other families with blankets and hot meals.

On *Monday* the Anglian Water Authority pumped the water from the Dodds' street. It smelled awful because of the sewage in it. On *Tuesday* the electrician isolated the sockets downstairs so that the electricity upstairs could be turned on. The assessor from the insurance

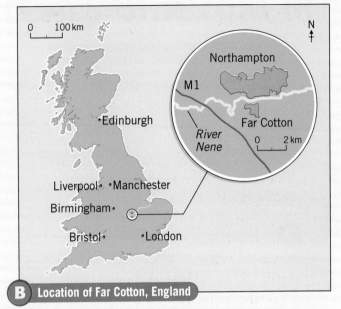

B | Location of Far Cotton, England

company came on the *Thursday* and agreed that they needed new carpets.

Over the *next three weeks* Fiona and Mark had to strip the floors down to bare concrete and take the plaster off the walls. Fiona found the constant noise of four dehumidifiers and air-movers very stressful. Their daily struggles with their insurance company and bank put them both under a huge strain.

Mark was critical about the lack of help from the local council: 'Since the flood, we have had no information on health and hygiene precautions or possible pollution effects, except for one leaflet telling us to wash our hands and wear rubber gloves!' He was also angry to discover that the Environment Agency, in charge of flood defences and warnings, had provided sandbags and boats to other flooded areas.

Three months after the flood Fiona and Mark were still shocked and angry: shocked that their lives could have been devastated by flood water sweeping away their possessions; angry that this could have happened without warning. All they could ask was: 'Why did this happen to us?' and 'Could it happen again?'

• *Based on information from the Environment Agency's Easter 1998 Flood report*

What caused the flooding in Mozambique?

AFRICA

A Mozambique fact file

Area: 801 590 square km (UK 244 100 square km)

Capital: Maputo

Population: 18 million (UK 56 million)

Language: Portuguese, but most people speak local languages, e.g. Swahili

Life expectancy: 47 years

Landscape: Mainly lowland with many large rivers

B

In February 2000 rainfall was much higher than usual for the rainy season. A total of 1163 mm of rain fell during the month compared with the average of 177 mm. The area around Maputo received 455 mm of rain in only 3 days. It led to the worst flooding in southern Mozambique for 40 years. Heavy rains also caused problems in Zimbabwe. Eight-metre-high waves rushed down the Limpopo and Incomati rivers and into Mozambique. As there was no warning system between the two countries the people of Mozambique could do nothing to prepare themselves.

C

By **February 20** the government announced that over 300 000 people had lost their homes. Then on **February 21** cyclone Eline hit southern Mozambique. It destroyed roads, ripped roofs off houses, cut electricity and telephone lines and increased the rainfall. In Zambia huge floods were caused when the overspill gates of the giant Kariba Dam were opened to stop them from bursting. Southern areas of Mozambique were worst affected with over 100 000 hectares of farm land flooded. People have since claimed that some farming and building methods may have made the floods worse.

Activities

1 Create a fact file for Mozambique using an atlas. Use the information in **A** as a starting point. Include information such as *average temperature*, *average rainfall*, *vegetation*, *wealth*, *land use*, *crops* and *population density*.

2 a The flooding between the cities of Maputo and Xai-Xai was at least 5 metres deep. Measure the distance in kilometres between these two cities.

b If this flooding had happened where you live, how far would it stretch? Name a place that is the same distance from your home as Maputo is from Xai-Xai.

3 Draw a table with two columns like the one below. Write in the *physical* and *human* causes of this flooding disaster.

Physical causes	Human causes

The effects of the floods in Mozambique

For two weeks, Joao Nhassengo had no idea whether his family was alive. He first heard of the floods in his own country of Mozambique on the radio at the Johannesburg gold mines where he works. With a one-week pass from work in hand, he rushed home, where he discovered his village underwater and his family gone.

When the water had dropped to waist deep he made his way back to his home, but there was still no word of his family. Then two days ago his wife, Beatriz, returned. 'When I saw her coming across the field on her own, I thought the children must be dead or very sick.' To his joy, he learned that the children had survived and were in a camp.

Now they are all together again. The children have stomach pains caused by drinking the polluted floodwater. Many of their neighbours have caught cholera from it. Their home is wrecked. The force of the water smashed all the windows and ripped the doors from their hinges. It tore away part of the roof.

But most important are the crops. Beatriz, who is 21, worked a patch of ground nearly five metres wide by 12 metres long. This land fed her family, and, if there was a good harvest, supplied a little extra cash. 'The hoes are still in the house. That is a start, but the maize is ruined.'

'It is something to survive. My children are alive. My house I can rebuild. My crops will grow again. There are many struggles in life. This is just one.'

Adapted from *The Guardian*, Friday 10 March, 2000

The TV cameras have gone but the misery goes on in Mozambique. The water wrecked or damaged the homes of about 250 000 people. Most factories were largely untouched by the floods. However, there was considerable damage to the roads and railways used for trade.

The government estimates that it will need £175 million to rebuild the 620 miles of roads and long stretches of railway track that were swept away. Then there are the electricity and telephone lines and more than 600 schools in need of repair.

**Adapted from *The Guardian*,
Tuesday 28 March, 2000**

A People abandon their homes taking only what they can carry

TREE PEOPLE FACE WILDLIFE PERIL

Celeste Limbombo said her clothes and head were covered in bugs for days. 'Sometimes I couldn't open my eyes because the insects crawled into them. There was no food and drinking the water made me sick. If you are in a tree you have to do all your private things in front of everybody. If you are young it is easy; you can climb down to the water. If you are old it is very hard to move.'

The Guardian, Saturday 4 March, 2000

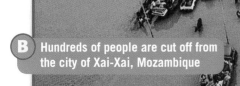

B Hundreds of people are cut off from the city of Xai-Xai, Mozambique

C Rescue arrives just in time for these flood victims, but they are the lucky ones

D A flooded village near to the Limpopo River, Mozambique

Forty-one helicopters and 15 planes flying from Maputo and Beira are transporting food and medical supplies. So far 14 000 people have been airlifted to safety by six South African helicopters. But there are too few to pluck all the survivors from the flood and many have lived in trees for days.

One helicopter pilot wept as he described his desperation at being able to save just a few dozen people at a time. 'People are just disappearing. We can't get to them all in time. We see people waving from the roofs of houses and when we fly back they're gone,' he said.

One woman threw her baby at a full helicopter as it lifted off. A crew member caught the child but the mother's fate is unknown.

Daily Telegraph, **Tuesday 29 March, 2000**

- The United Nations has appealed for £9.1 million in emergency aid for Mozambique.
- Britain has donated £5.8 million and cancelled Mozambique's debts.
- British aid included 100 boats and life rafts, 30 emergency rescue workers, a military team, four RAF helicopters and money to hire further helicopters.
- The charities Action Aid, Save the Children, Oxfam, Cafod, Christian Aid, Red Cross, Concern, Help the Aged, Merlin, Tear Fund and World Vision have all helped.
- Italy provided £3.3 million in aid and Japan gave £62,500 in tents and equipment.
- The French relief agency Médecins du Monde sent a five-person team and 10 tonnes of medical equipment.

Activities

1. Draw a very large Venn diagram like the one opposite. On the diagram write in:
   - the effects of flooding in the *United Kingdom*, in *Mozambique* and in *both countries* in one colour
   - people's responses to the flooding in the *United Kingdom*, in *Mozambique* and in *both countries* in a second colour.

   Draw a key for the two colours.

2. Use the information in your Venn diagram to write a comparison of the flooding in the United Kingdom and in Mozambique. You should include two side-headings:
   The effects of flooding in the United Kingdom and in Mozambique and
   People's responses to the flooding in the United Kingdom and in Mozambique.
   Under each heading you should mention the *similarities* and *differences* between the two places.

How to...

... draw a Venn diagram

1. Draw two interlocking circles, large enough to write in, as shown below.

2. Label each circle. In this case, use United Kingdom and Mozambique.

3. Write the names of any shared effects and responses in the overlapping sections.

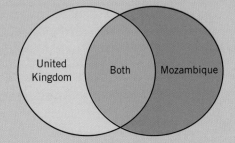

United Kingdom — Both — Mozambique

Review and reflect

Flood disaster – how do people cope?

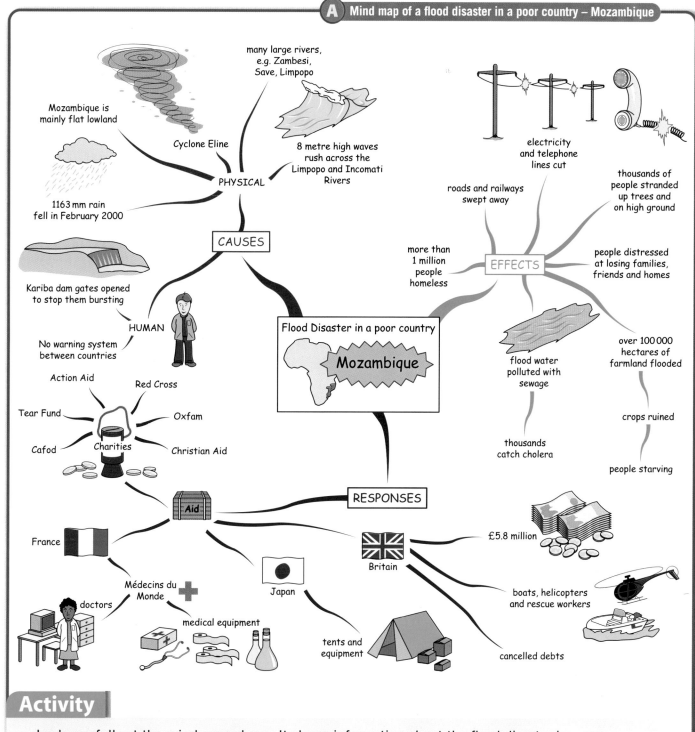

A Mind map of a flood disaster in a poor country – Mozambique

Activity

Look carefully at the mind map above. It shows information about the flood disaster in Mozambique – a poor country. Use it as a model to draw a similar mind map for the United Kingdom – a rich country.

Use information from pages 132–137 of this book as a starting point. If you are able to, add facts from research you have done.

8 Can the Earth cope?

Ecosystems, population and resources

A Smoke emissions in New Orleans, USA

B Marine pollution at the island of Tiree, Scotland

C Deforestation in Johor State, Malaysia

D Rock slide following an earthquake, India

Learn about

The world's growing population and its demand for resources have many consequences for the environment. This unit will help you investigate ecosystems, population and resources, and how they are linked together. You will explore:

- what ecosystems are and where they are found
- how vegetation is related to climate, soil and human activity
- how population and resources are linked
- how a resource can best be managed
- what the future is for global resources.

E Confiscated ivory being burned in Kenya

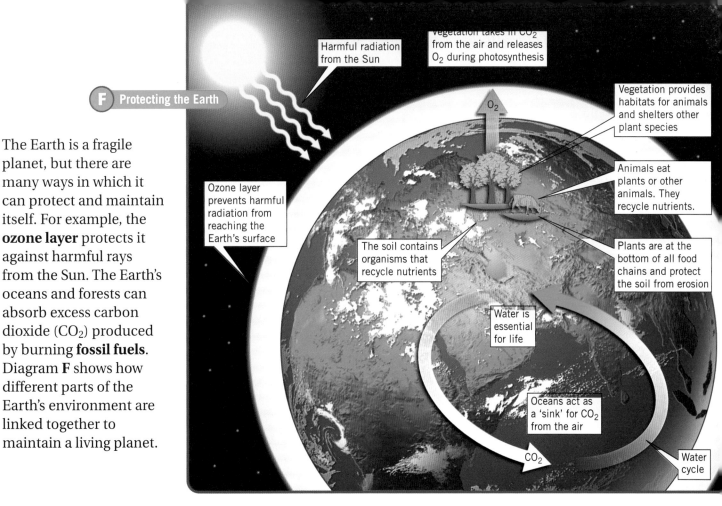

Harmful radiation from the Sun

Vegetation takes in CO₂ from the air and releases O₂ during photosynthesis

Vegetation provides habitats for animals and shelters other plant species

Ozone layer prevents harmful radiation from reaching the Earth's surface

Animals eat plants or other animals. They recycle nutrients.

The soil contains organisms that recycle nutrients

Plants are at the bottom of all food chains and protect the soil from erosion

Water is essential for life

Oceans act as a 'sink' for CO₂ from the air

O_2 CO_2 **Water cycle**

The Earth is a fragile planet, but there are many ways in which it can protect and maintain itself. For example, the **ozone layer** protects it against harmful rays from the Sun. The Earth's oceans and forests can absorb excess carbon dioxide (CO_2) produced by burning **fossil fuels**. Diagram **F** shows how different parts of the Earth's environment are linked together to maintain a living planet.

However, how can the Earth continue to cope with the increasing pressure put on it by human beings? The world's population continues to grow at an alarming rate: approximately 1.6 million more people a week in 2001. This growing population consumes more and more of the Earth's resources, for food, clothing and shelter, as well as to make a huge range of other goods.

Activities

① In a small group, discuss ways in which the Earth is able to protect itself. Diagram **F** will help you. Use the points in the table, as well as adding your own.

Parts of the environment	How they help to protect and maintain the Earth
Vegetation (**flora**)	
Soil	
Water	
Animals (**fauna**)	
The atmosphere	

③ **Extension**

Investigate environmental incidents in the news using newspapers, TV or the Internet. Add them to your list in **2**, then present a summary of your findings. You can find useful information by following the links on www.heinemann.co.uk/hotlinks (code 5430P). (ICT)

② Study the environmental incidents shown in the photographs, and use an atlas to find their locations. Then copy and complete this table.

Photograph and what it shows	Country where the incident took place	Continent	Populated area (Yes or No)	Part of the Earth *most* affected (vegetation, soil, water, animals, atmosphere)
A				
B				

Where are the Earth's major ecosystems?

The Earth is made up of many different **ecosystems**. Map **A** shows the world distribution of three types of ecosystems: tropical rainforest ecosystems, hot desert ecosystems and coral reef ecosystems. An ecosystem on a global scale is often referred to as a **biome**.

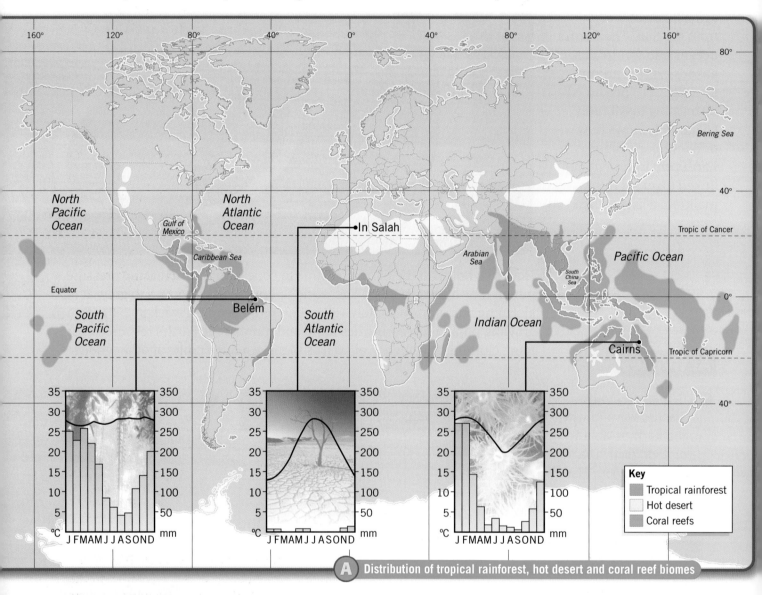

A Distribution of tropical rainforest, hot desert and coral reef biomes

Getting Technical ▼

- An **ecosystem** is a community of plants and animals and the environment they live in. Each part of the ecosystem depends on the other parts. An ecosystem includes **flora** (plants), **fauna** (animals), climate and soil.
- A **biome** is the biggest ecological unit. It consists of a group of related ecosystems that share the same kind of special plant life and climate.
- A **community** is a group of plants and animals living closely together.

How does vegetation adapt to its environment?

Plants develop special features to survive and make the most of their environment. These features are called **adaptations**. They allow a plant to cope with too much water or too little, too much heat or cold, windy or calm conditions. The diagrams in **B** show some examples of adaptations made by plants in a variety of biomes.

Spines of a cactus plant – in dry climates, these lose less water through **evapotranspiration** than leaves.

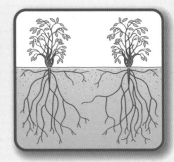

Long root systems just beneath the soil – plants in hot, dry environments need to use any rain that falls immediately.

Buttress roots – in a tropical rainforest, trees grow to great heights to compete for sunlight and air. The large buttress roots support the tall trees.

Leaves with **drip tips** – in very wet climates the drip tips allow rainwater to run off the leaf quickly, before the plant is damaged by the weight of water that may collect.

B These plants show adaptations to a variety of environmental conditions

Activities

1. In pairs, investigate either tropical rainforest or hot desert in more detail. Follow these steps and use **A** to prepare a guide to your biome.
   a Describe its world distribution.
   b Use an atlas to find three named examples of your chosen biome.
   c Name the continents or oceans and some countries where the biome is found. It may be on the land or in the waters around those countries.
   d Use the photograph in **A** to describe or sketch the vegetation.
   e Use the graph in **A** to describe the climate at different times of the year.

2. a Design and draw a perfect plant that would flourish in your chosen biome. Use the adaptations shown in **B** as a starting point.

help!

Try to use some of these terms in your answers:
- ❂ Northern Hemisphere/ Southern Hemisphere
- ❂ Equator
- ❂ Tropics
- ❂ coastal
- ❂ interior
- ❂ even/uneven
- ❂ scattered
- ❂ clustered.

   b Annotate your diagram to show how your plant would adapt to the conditions in the biome. Think about the difficulties it may face from the climate, other flora, fauna and the soil.

3. **Extension**

   Find the map of world vegetation in your atlas. Choose a different biome to investigate and compare it to your work in activity **1**.

How are ecosystems linked to human activity?

An ecosystem is a **community** of plants and animals which exist together under similar conditions, such as climate and soil. Diagram **A** helps you to understand what an ecosystem is and how the four parts of an ecosystem are closely interconnected.

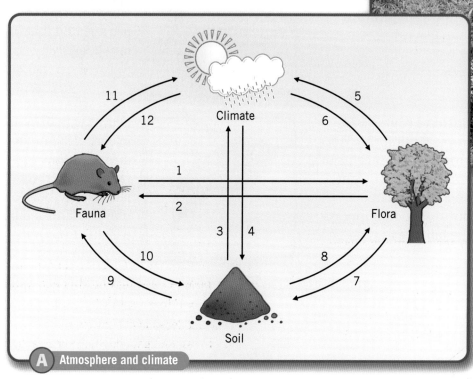

A Atmosphere and climate

B The Amazonian rainforest ecosystem

Most ecosystems are affected by human activity. People need to use and modify the natural environment to help them survive, for example to grow food, provide shelter, or extract resources such as coal or precious metals. Activity **3** will help you explore these **impacts**. However, if the Earth is to cope with the demands that are made on it, people need to realise that many of its resources are not renewable – they will run out. Humans will have to use and manage the Earth's resources in a more **sustainable** way.

Getting Technical ▼

- **Renewable resource:** a resource which can be used again and again, for example trees, which can be replanted, or wind, which can be used to make electricity
- **Non-renewable resource:** a resource which will never be replaced once it is used, for example soil

- **Sustainable development:** using resources wisely today, so that people in the future can still use them. To be sustainable, renewable resources must be allowed to regenerate, and alternatives must be found for non-renewable resources

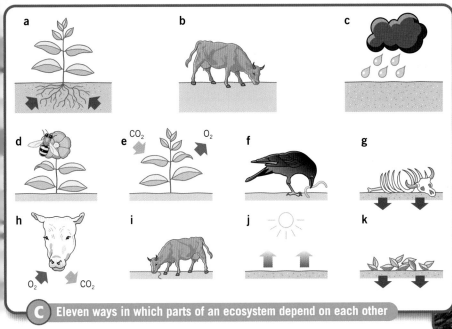

C Eleven ways in which parts of an ecosystem depend on each other

D Human impacts on ecosystem in Amazonia

Activities

1 **a** Draw a sketch of a tropical rainforest.

b Use diagram **A** to label the four main parts of the ecosystem on your sketch.

c Add arrows copied from diagram **A** to show how the different parts of the ecosystem are linked.

2 Look at diagram **A** and the sketches in **C**.

a Make a copy of the table below.

b Match the sketches **a–k** in **C** to the numbered arrows 1 to 12 in **A**. Some sketches match two numbers.

c Describe what each link shows.

d Write a short summary of what you have found out about ecosystems.

Arrow number (1–12)	Matches with sketch (a–k)	Description of the link
1	d	A bee pollinates the flower of a plant
2		

3 Photograph **D** shows the effects of human activity on an ecosystem.

a Work in pairs at first for this activity. First discuss which ecosystem is shown in **D**, and how human activity has changed it. It may help you to write notes on rough paper.

b Use diagram **A** to discuss how changes will affect the fauna, flora, soil and climate in this ecosystem.

For example:

> By cutting down the trees, people have removed protection from the soil. This allows rain to wash the soil away …

c Write a paragraph to describe and explain the impact people have had on this ecosystem. Include the following information:

- ⊚ name and location of ecosystem
- ⊚ the change brought about by human activity
- ⊚ the effects on fauna
- ⊚ the effects on flora
- ⊚ the effects on soil
- ⊚ the effects on climate.

help!

Remember that:

- ✿ good descriptions include details or examples
- ✿ good explanations say why things change – they use linking words like *why*, *because*, and *so*.

4 Humans need to use ecosystems to survive. Try to think of ways in which we can use the Earth's ecosystems while causing as little damage as possible. You could start by thinking of how to use the ecosystem in photograph **D** in a more sustainable way.

How do ecosystems work?

All living things need energy to exist. Animals such as humans get their energy by eating plants or other animals, but plants can make their own energy. They take water from the soil, and use carbon dioxide from the atmosphere and sunlight to produce the energy they need. This process takes place in the green leaves of plants and is called **photosynthesis**.

Photosynthesis happens faster where there is plenty of sunlight, high temperatures and enough moisture. So photosynthesis produces more energy in some parts of the world than in others, and plants are able to grow faster (photos **D–H**).

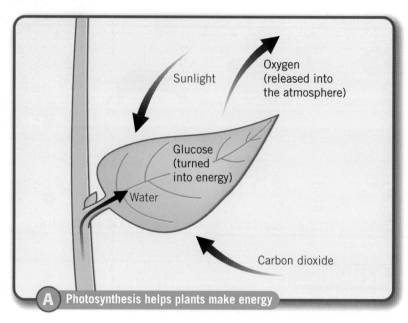

Sunlight

Oxygen (released into the atmosphere)

Glucose (turned into energy)

Water

Carbon dioxide

A Photosynthesis helps plants make energy

The energy plants produce is essential to other living things. Some animals get their energy from eating plants, and they are eaten by other animals. So the energy plants make flows through a **food chain** to other parts of the ecosystem (see **B**).

The total amount of energy plants produce in an ecosystem is called **primary productivity**. Ecosystems with high productivity have more species of plants and animals, because there is more energy available to support them.

How nutrients are recycled

Plants and animals need **nutrients** as well as energy to grow. Plants take nutrients from the soil through their roots. These nutrients move through the food chain and are recycled back into the soil. For example, when plants and animals die, they are broken down by bacteria and fungi (see **C**). Nutrients are recycled much more quickly in parts of the world with warm, wet climates than in cold or dry climates. Where nutrients are recycled quickly, they are stored in the vegetation, and the soils can become poor.

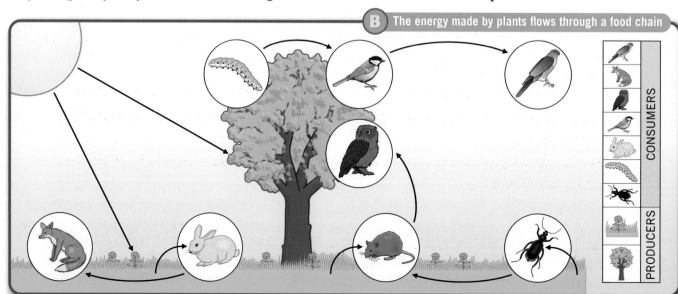

B The energy made by plants flows through a food chain

CONSUMERS

PRODUCERS

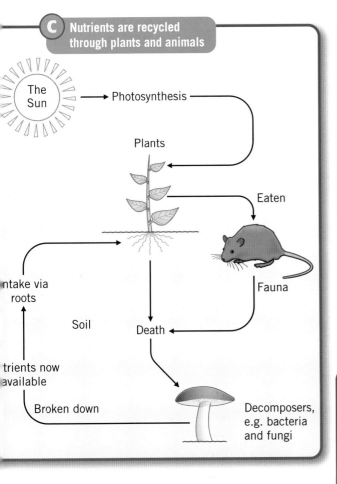

C Nutrients are recycled through plants and animals

The Sun → Photosynthesis

Plants

Eaten

Fauna

Intake via roots

Soil

Death

Nutrients now available

Broken down

Decomposers, e.g. bacteria and fungi

D Tropical rainforest

E Hot desert

F Temperate grassland

H Tundra

G Tropical savannah

Activities

1. **a** On a copy of figure **A**, underline the inputs to photosynthesis in one colour, and the outputs in a different colour.

   b Next to each input, label where the plant gets it from.

   c Now write a sentence or two explaining the process of photosynthesis in your own words.

2. **a** Find a world map of vegetation types in your atlas. Find the ecosystems shown in photographs **D** to **H**.

   b Make a list of the ecosystems. You could set your work out in a table like the one below.

   c Study the photographs and find out about their climates. Decide which ecosystems will have the highest rate of photosynthesis.

Ecosystem	Climate	Photosynthesis	Reasons
Tropical rainforest	Hot and wet most of the year	High	High temperatures and rainfall

   d Now decide which ecosystems will have low or medium rates of photosynthesis. Explain your choices.

3. Choose ecosystems from photographs **D** to **H** where you think nutrient cycling would be fast, medium or slow.

4. Check that you understand the definitions of the key words in **bold**, then add them to your geography word bank.

5. **Extension**

   Write a short summary explaining what you have found out about how ecosystems in different parts of the world work, or label what you have found out onto a world map.

149

How are population and resources linked?

As you have seen, the world's growing population uses more and more of the Earth's resources. However, people in different parts of the world do not have equal access to the world's natural resources. For example:

- ◎ the richest 20 per cent of the world's population use 80 per cent of the resources
- ◎ the richest 20 per cent of the world's population own 85 per cent of the wealth
- ◎ 80 per cent of the world's population live in LEDCs.

One reason is that natural resources are not found evenly throughout the world (**C**). Another is that wealthier countries have the power and money to gain a bigger share of the world's resources through trade. For example, wealthy countries such as Japan with few natural resources buy resources from poorer countries with more resources. The population of the USA uses more of the Earth's resources than any other country. Unlike Japan, it has many resources of its own.

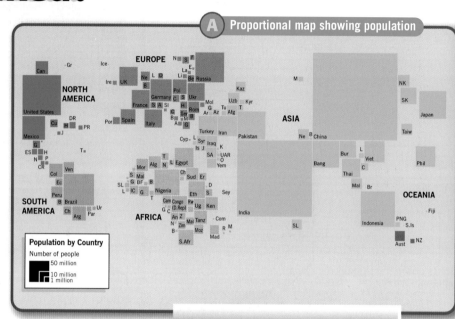

A Proportional map showing population

Getting Technical ▼

Proportional maps

A **proportional map** uses a value, such as GDP, to map the world, rather than land area. So Switzerland, which looks small on a traditional map, looks big because it has a high GNP.

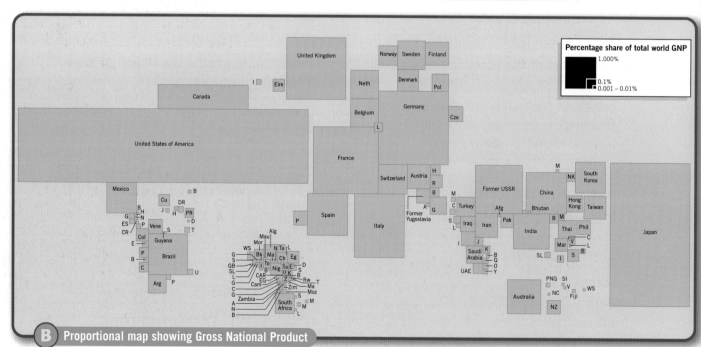

B Proportional map showing Gross National Product

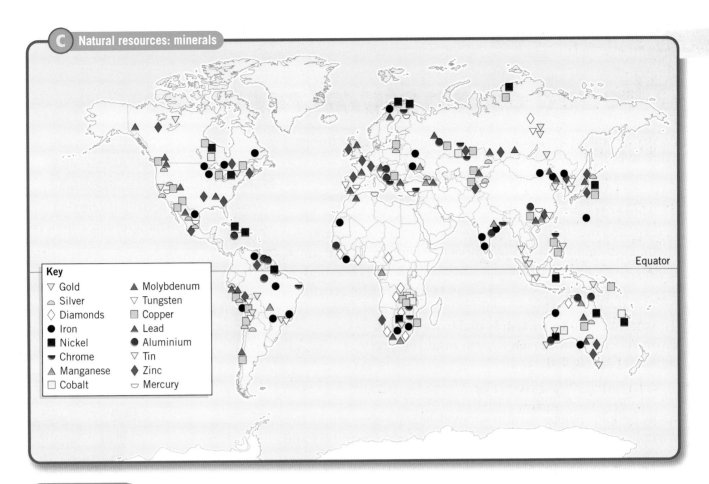

Key

▽ Gold	▲ Molybdenum
⌂ Silver	▽ Tungsten
◇ Diamonds	▢ Copper
● Iron	▲ Lead
■ Nickel	⬤ Aluminium
⬮ Chrome	▽ Tin
△ Manganese	◆ Zinc
▢ Cobalt	⌣ Mercury

Equator

Activities

1 The purpose of this activity is to get you thinking about natural resources. Work in pairs.

  a Think carefully about a room at home or in school. Imagine you are taking a video camera into the room. Pan the camera around the room and think of all the objects you can see. It may help if you close your eyes.

  b In turn, describe what you saw to your partner while they note all the objects down.

  c Discuss which natural resources were used to make each object. List them next to the object.

> **help!** Some household goods include hundreds of parts made of many different resources. You could aim for variety in your list, or investigate one object in more detail. You could then share your ideas with the rest of the class to get one large list.

2 Discuss which resources are **renewable** and which are **non-renewable**. Colour code your list into these two groups.

3 Use maps **A** and **B** and an atlas to find:

  ◉ a wealthy region of the world with a high population

  ◉ a poor region of the world with a high population

  ◉ a poor region of the world with a low population

  ◉ a wealthy part of the world with a low population.

4 Work in pairs or groups of three.

  a Choose one resource each from map **C**, and investigate the distribution of the resource – use these questions to help you.

  ◉ Which continents or countries is it mainly found in?

  ◉ Which parts of the world lack the resource?

  ◉ Is the resource found in parts of the world where many people live?

  ◉ Is the resource found in parts of the world which have a high, medium or low GDP?

  b Compare your results with those of your partner. What are the main similarities and differences between the resources?

  c Produce a world outline map showing the distribution of your resources. Annotate it to show your findings.

5 Add the key words in **bold** on these two pages to your word bank. 📖

The sea as a natural resource

As you have already discovered, natural resources are things you use every day. They can be found above ground, underground, in the air and in water. These two pages investigate the natural resources of our seas and oceans.

Almost 71 per cent of the Earth's surface is covered by the oceans, and over 97 per cent of the Earth's water is stored in them. The oceans have a huge impact on climate around the globe. They supply water which reaches the land as rain and snow, and influence the temperature and winds. The oceans are also the home of huge numbers of animals and plants. The **marine** (sea) ecosystem is vital to the Earth's environment – without it the Earth would be a very different place to live.

Like all the Earth's resources, marine ecosystems are fragile and under threat from human activity. However, they are also vital for many people's livelihood and survival. Marine ecosystems support a whole range of economic activities, **primary**, **secondary** and **tertiary**. Even for people who do not have direct contact with the sea, it is an important resource.

Photographs **A–F** show a variety of ways in which people use marine ecosystems as a resource.

Getting Technical ▼

- A **primary** activity is one that takes a natural resource from the Earth.
- A **secondary** activity is one that makes a product from resources.
- A **tertiary** activity provides a service to people.

C Japanese whaling in the Southern Ocean

A Ayrshire coast, Scotland, seaside view

D An oil rig in the North Sea

B Fishing trawler, Bering Sea

E Diving off the coast of Kenya

F Fish grading in Orkney, Scotland

Activities

1 **a** With a partner, study photographs **A** to **F**, then discuss the different ways they show people using the sea as a resource.

b Copy the table below. For each photograph, describe at least one way in which the sea is being used.

c Decide whether each activity is primary, secondary or tertiary, then add an explanation to your table. One example has been done for you.

hint

Be careful – there may not be a simple answer for some of these photographs. It all depends on the reason you give.

Photograph	Location	How the sea is used as a resource	Primary, secondary or tertiary activity
F	Scotland	The photo shows the sea is being used as a source of food for people.	This is a secondary activity because the fish will be made into products like fish cakes.

2 **a** Work in pairs. Choose three of the photographs you have investigated. Work out ways in which the activities they show may have an impact on the marine ecosystem. Share your ideas with another pair.

b Using the photographs to help you, list the ways you or your families use the sea as a resource. Are there any links between your use of the resources and impacts on the environment?

3 Use the photographs and your work so far to look for resource chains that link natural resources and the people who consume them. You can see one example, partly complete, in the table. Try to think of at least one more.

Resource	Primary activity	Secondary activity	Tertiary activity	Consumer
Fish		Fish factory		People eating fish products

4 Use the Oceans Alive website (follow the links on www.heinemann.co.uk/hotlinks (code 5430P)) and other resources from a library or newspapers to produce a leaflet or poster explaining to the reader how and why the sea is an important resource. You could use a wordprocessing or DTP package to present your work. (ICT)

Threats to marine ecosystems

Seas and oceans cover over two-thirds of the Earth's surface, so it is not surprising that they have become polluted as a result of human activities. Polluted water and waste materials are dumped directly into the sea, flow into the sea from rivers, or fall from the atmosphere. Table **A** shows the main sources of marine pollution.

Source		Pollutants	Percentage of total
Atmosphere		Particles blown by the wind, and gases from industry and vehicles	33%
Run-off and discharges from the land		Sewage and waste from farms and industry	44%
Ships		Oil spills and leaks, and cargo spills	12%
Dumping at sea		Waste from dredging, sewage sludge, and ships' garbage	10%
Offshore oil and gas production		Waste from oil and gas drilling	1%

A Sources of marine pollution

People are often surprised that oil spills make up such a small percentage of marine pollution. When an oil spill occurs, it is very visible and some of the impacts are almost immediate. However, run-off and discharges from the land are more widespread and are harder to trace.

The oil industry

Oil is one of the most valuable resources which people **extract** from the environment. **Crude oil** was formed many millions of years ago, so it is a **non-renewable resource**. It is found in rocks beneath the land and some of the Earth's seas.

As well as extracting oil from the seas and oceans, we also transport oil by sea to where it will be **refined** and used. Pipelines and huge tankers carry oil across the world. Map **C** shows the world's major oilfields and the network of oil shipping lanes which link the producers of oil with the countries which **consume** it. However, producing and transporting oil puts the world's marine ecosystems at risk from oil pollution (see **B**).

Getting Technical

- **Pollution:** when harmful substances make the air, land or water dirty
- **Pollutant:** a harmful substance that causes pollution, such as exhaust fumes.

Sea animals and birds may swallow the oil and be poisoned.

Animals and birds may freeze to death when their fur or feathers get matted with oil.

Some species are poisoned by oil fumes.

Floating oil contaminates plankton.

Predators may starve because fish contaminated by oil taste and smell unpleasant.

Oil contaminates fish eggs.

Spilled oil may stop the marine plants from growing.

Marine life on reefs or shorelines is smothered as oil is washed ashore.

B Effects of oil on the marine ecosystem

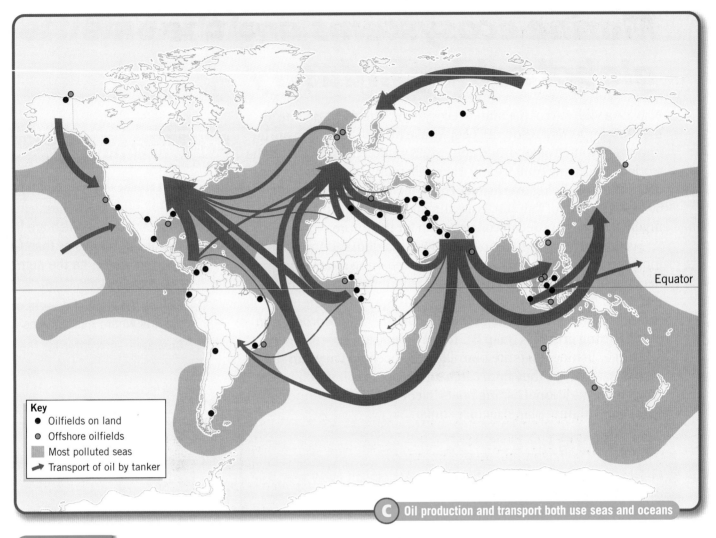

Key
- Oilfields on land
- Offshore oilfields
- Most polluted seas
- Transport of oil by tanker

C Oil production and transport both use seas and oceans

Activities

1 Draw a graph to show the data in table **A**. Choose the type of graph you use carefully. Add a title and a key.

2 Study diagram **B**, which shows the impact of oil on a marine ecosystem.

  a Choose the impact that you think would affect the marine ecosystem most quickly. Explain your choice.

  b Which of the impacts do you think would take the longest to affect the marine ecosystem?

3 Use map **C** and an atlas to investigate the seas and oceans where the threat of oil pollution is greatest.

  a Find the world's biggest oil-producing area, and the three parts of the world which consume most oil.

  b List the seas or oceans where offshore oilfields are located.

  c List the oceans and seas most at risk from accidents or spills from oil tankers.

4 Map **C** also shows the most polluted seas in the world.

  a Working in pairs, see whether you can see a link between the pattern of polluted seas and what you have found out about the risk of oil pollution. You might want to make a rough list of seas where there seems to be a link, and a list of seas where there does not seem to be a link.

  b Make a short presentation of your conclusions. Table **A** may help you explain what you have found out.

  c Look through the other world maps in your atlas. Find another map which helps you to explain more about the pattern of marine pollution.

Marine ecosystems and the global fishing industry

Fish are a vital part of the marine ecosystem. They are also one of the most important resources people take from the sea. Fish are an important source of food, and about 12.5 million people around the world earn a living from fishing. However, many of the world's seas and oceans are being **overfished**. The United Nations believe that 60 to 70 per cent of **fish stocks** are threatened worldwide, and urgent action is needed to **conserve** fish for the future.

As the world's population has grown, the demand for fish has increased rapidly. At the same time, many fishing boats have become better at catching fish, so the amount of fish caught has increased too (graph **A**). But although fish is a **renewable** resource, fish are being caught faster than they can reproduce in many **fishing grounds** (map **B**). To make matters worse, newer and larger fishing boats are patrolling the oceans. They can sail to distant seas where they find, catch and process fish much more efficiently. Traditional fishing boats in coastal waters cannot compete with these large factory ships.

Getting Technical

- **Fish stock:** the total number of fish in an area
- **Overfishing:** when fish are taken out of the sea faster than they can reproduce, so the number of fish steadily goes down
- **Fishing grounds:** the parts of the oceans where fishing goes on
- **Conserve:** look after for the future

Fact file

- People in Japan eat the most fish: 72 kg per person every year.
- Other big fish-eaters are the people of Iceland and Greenland.
- The four biggest fishing nations are China, Peru, Chile and Japan. They take 42 per cent of the world's fishing catch.

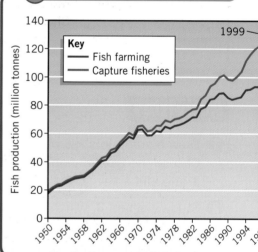

A World fish production, 1950–1999

B The world's fishing grounds

Barents Sea, Grand Banks, Bahamian Marine Ecosystem, Southern Caribbean Sea, North East Brazilian Coastal Ecosystem, Mediterranean Sea, Gulf of Guinea Marine Ecosystems, Western Guinea Current Marine Ecosystem, Equator, South West Atlantic Coast Marine Ecosystem

Key Fish consumption per person per year: 0–10 kg, 11–30 kg, 31–50 kg, 51–80 kg, Threatened fisheries, Fishing grounds

Ocean	Fish catch in million tonnes
North Atlantic	21
South Atlantic	4
Indian	8
Western Pacific	34.3
Eastern Pacific	18.9

C The world fish catch, 1997

Traditional fishing boats often fish quite close to land, and provide jobs for local people. They are usually too small to overfish, so they are more **sustainable** (photo **D**).

Factory ships (photo **E**) track fish down using electronic equipment and catch them using huge nets. The fish are often processed and frozen on board.

One solution to overfishing is to raise fish in fish farms (photo **F**). The fish are specially fed so they grow fast. When they are big enough, they are easy to catch. However, the waste from fish farms can pollute the surrounding water.

D Traditional fishing in Kerala, India

E Processing fish aboard a trawler in the Bering Sea

F Salmon farm in Dover, Tasmania

Activities

1 a Use the figures in table **C** and an outline map of the world. Choose a type of graph to show the weight of fish caught in each ocean. (123)

b Shade your map to show the endangered fishing grounds.

c Label the information in the fact file onto your map.

d In pairs, discuss whether you can see any links between the different sorts of information on your map.

2 a Read again about traditional fishing, modern factory ships and fish farming and look at photographs **D**, **E** and **F**. Draw up a table like the one below to help you work out the advantages and disadvantages of each sort of fishing.

	Advantages	Disadvantages
Traditional fishing boats		
Large factory ships		
Fish farming		

b Underline the advantages and disadvantages for people in blue, and those for the environment in green.

3 Using your work from activities **1** and **2**, write a short summary to explain what you have learned about the problem of overfishing. Include all the key words in **bold** to show you understand them.

4 **Extension**

Investigate overfishing and conservation from the Worldwide Fund for Nature website. Go to www.heinemann.co.uk/hotlinks and key in code 5430P. Choose either **a** or **b** below.

a Choose one fishing problem or conservation story from the website. Make an ICT presentation by choosing images and key points from the website.

b Use an atlas to check the location of the main news stories and annotate them onto a world outline map. Then colour code your labels to show different types of story, for example problems and successes. (ICT)

Case Study

Overfishing in the North Sea

A The North Sea

The North Sea is suffering the effects of overfishing. Scientists warn that cod numbers in the North Sea are about to collapse. The World Wide Fund for Nature (WWF) go further – they say that in some places cod is actually an **endangered species**.

One reason for this is that most of the big fish have already been caught. As cod becomes harder to find, fishermen are forced to catch smaller and younger fish. Eighty per cent of the cod they catch are below breeding age, leaving fewer and fewer cod to breed for the future.

The European Union

The countries around the North Sea all belong to the European Union (EU). The EU has a difficult job; it has to:

- manage fishing fairly for the fishermen of each country
- manage fishing in a sustainable way
- help keep people in the EU supplied with fish.

There are so few mackerel it is not worth fishermen leaving port. Herring are now recovering after numbers went so low in 1995 that fishing for them was banned. Cod, haddock, plaice and prawns are heading the same way. However, this does not have to be the case. During the First and Second World Wars no fishing took place in the North Sea. For five years after the wars finished, all fish species saw healthy recoveries. This could happen again!

B The views of Amy Chang, North Sea environmentalist

Even before the fishing ban, we were struggling to make ends meet. I understand the need for conservation, but I need to catch 170 tonnes of cod a year to make a profit. Three years ago I invested £250 000 in my trawler, but our catches have gone down for the past two years. I now travel further in search of fishing grounds where I am allowed to fish, towards the coast of Holland. This will increase my costs and I'll have to be out at sea longer. This ban is too harsh and the government should compensate us.

C Sam Douglas, fisherman from the Port of Grimsby

Saving the cod

Ban on North Sea cod fishing – 24 January 2001

THE EUROPEAN COMMISSION announces that 100 000 square kilometres of the North Sea, almost 20 per cent of its entire area, will be out of bounds to boats fishing for cod, haddock, and whiting. This is a desperate attempt to ensure that there will be cod left in the North Sea next year.

The UK will be worst affected by the ban since it has the longest coastline bordering the North Sea. Britain also has a long tradition of cod fishing – British people eat one-third of the world's cod catch.

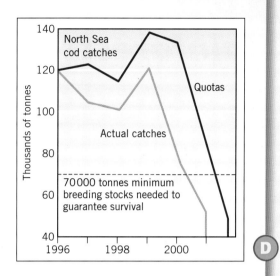

D

Conservation choices

Most people think conserving fish is a good idea, but it means making difficult decisions. These affect everybody who catches, processes or eats fish. The decisions also affect the future of the whole marine ecosystem. Ideas for conservation include:

- banning fishing from some areas of the North Sea
- a **quota** (limit) on the amount of fish that people can catch
- paying fishermen to scrap older boats
- limiting the number of days that fishermen can go fishing.

Activities

1 List the countries that border the North Sea which might want to fish there.

2 Look at figure **D**.

  a Describe what the graph tells you about changes in North Sea cod catches.

  b When was the last time fishermen matched the quota set by the EU? What does this tell you about cod numbers in the North Sea?

3 **a** Work in pairs. Make a list of the ideas for conservation in the North Sea, then explain how they would work. Make notes in a table like the one below.

Conservation ideas	How they would work	Ranking	Ranking
Banning fishing from some areas	This would help conserve fish because ...		

  b Decide which you think would be the best idea from the point of view of fishermen. Use a blue pen and rank this idea 1, then the next best 2, and so on.

  c Decide which you think would be the best idea from the point of view of the environmentalist. Use a green pen, and rank this idea 1, then the next best 2, and so on.

  d Make a short presentation to explain *your* point of view. Include any ideas of your own.

Coral reefs: the 'tropical rainforests' of the sea

A Aerial view of Kuata Island, south west of Fiji

B Stone coral

Coral reefs are one of the most important ecosystems in the world. They are very **diverse** – they are home to huge numbers of different fauna and flora. Many **ecologists** call them the 'tropical rainforests' of the sea because they provide a unique habitat. Although coral reefs cover less than 1 per cent of the Earth's surface, over 25 per cent of all fish species in the ocean live in, or close to, coral reefs.

What is a coral reef?

A coral reef is made up of millions upon millions of coral **polyps**. They are the thin living layer which covers the reef. The polyps are tiny animals, but they contain plants called **algae**. The algae use photosynthesis to convert sunlight into energy – this energy is used by the coral itself. Coral reefs are very colourful because many different algae reflect different colours in the sunlight.

The coral polyps make hard calcium carbonate. Over thousands of years this builds up and forms the massive reefs seen in places like the Great Barrier Reef in Australia.

Getting Technical ▼

6 **Biodiversity:** the number of different species of plants and animals in an ecosystem. Human activity has reduced the world's biodiversity, with some species of plants and animals becoming extinct.

C Conditions that encourage coral growth

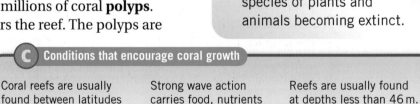

Coral reefs are usually found between latitudes 30° N and 30° S.

Strong wave action carries food, nutrients and oxygen to the reef.

Reefs are usually found at depths less than 46 m.

Coral polyps

Coral reef

Coral reefs need warm water – 20–28° C.

Reefs grow faster in clear water that allows more sunlight to penetrate.

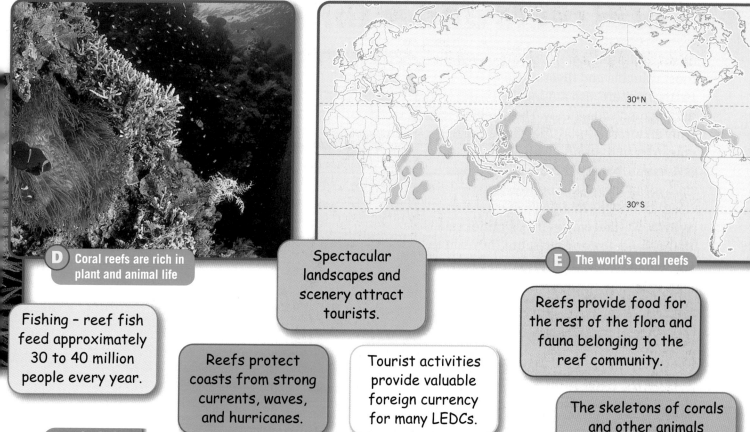

D Coral reefs are rich in plant and animal life

Spectacular landscapes and scenery attract tourists.

E The world's coral reefs

Reefs provide food for the rest of the flora and fauna belonging to the reef community.

Fishing – reef fish feed approximately 30 to 40 million people every year.

Reefs protect coasts from strong currents, waves, and hurricanes.

Tourist activities provide valuable foreign currency for many LEDCs.

The skeletons of corals and other animals provide sediments that create beaches.

Activities

1 Some people say coral reefs are like the tropical rainforests of the sea.

a Make a copy of the table below. Then put each of the words and phrases beneath the table in the correct column. The information on page 144 may help you.

Coral reefs only	Tropical rainforests only	Both coral reefs and tropical rainforests

- Located within the tropics
- Colourful
- Rich in animal and plant life
- Create spectacular scenery
- Take many years to grow and mature
- Use photosynthesis to make energy
- Are under threat from human activity
- Provide work for local people
- Protect the soil
- Shelter fish
- Easy to find out about in newspapers, magazines, and on TV

b Which, if any, did you find difficult to place in your table? Briefly explain your answer.

c Think of some words and phrases of your own to add to your table.

d Do you think that 'tropical rainforests of the sea' is a helpful description of coral reefs?

2 Using the Internet and other sources, collect information on different coral reefs around the world. Compare them by completing a table like the one below. You could add columns of your own to this table. Follow the links on www.heinemann.co.uk/hotlinks using code 5430P. **ICT**

Location of coral reef	Main features / Description of coral reef	Main threats to the coral reef

Coral reefs under threat

As we have seen, coral reefs are one of the most valuable and **diverse** ecosystems on Earth. They are also among the most endangered ecosystems. The threat is truly an international one. There are 109 countries in the world with a coral reef ecosystem. Ninety-three of these report damage to their reefs, or even destruction. The main culprit is human activity. Natural causes play a minor role in the threat to coral reefs, but they add to the damage caused by human activity.

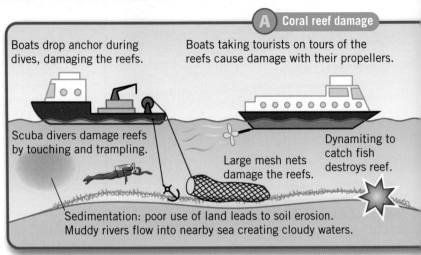

A Coral reef damage

Boats drop anchor during dives, damaging the reefs.

Boats taking tourists on tours of the reefs cause damage with their propellers.

Scuba divers damage reefs by touching and trampling.

Large mesh nets damage the reefs.

Dynamiting to catch fish destroys reef.

Sedimentation: poor use of land leads to soil erosion. Muddy rivers flow into nearby sea creating cloudy waters.

Natural threat to coral reef	Summary of threat
The effects of climate change	Changes in weather patterns cause problems for reef ecosystems. Hurricanes have been stronger and more frequent recently, which may be partly due to global warming. Storms have devastating effects on the coral reefs because of the increase in wave energy. Also sediment generated during storms can bury whole coral communities.
The effects of changes in sea level	Coral reefs need sunlight, but as sea levels rise this is reduced by the deeper water above them. Sea levels have risen by 10–25 cm over the past century, and are forecast to rise 15–95 cm over the next. Quick-growing species can keep pace with sea level rises but slow-growing species need shallow water.
Rise in sea temperatures	Sea temperatures may be increasing by about 1–2 °C per century. Coral reefs can only grow within a certain temperature range. Above this, corals deteriorate and may die. This is known as *coral bleaching*.

B Natural threats to coral reefs

Coral reefs – a magnet for tourism

Tourism is the world's fastest growing industry. Coral reefs are a resource that attracts large numbers of tourists from around the world to places like the Caribbean. One hundred million visitors flock to the Caribbean every year, earning 40 per cent of the region's Gross National Product (GNP).

The sheer beauty of coral reefs is just one of the attractions for the visitor. Scuba diving is increasingly popular and allows the tourist to get a close look at this diverse ecosystem and its varied marine life. Unfortunately, it also directly affects the health of coral reefs.

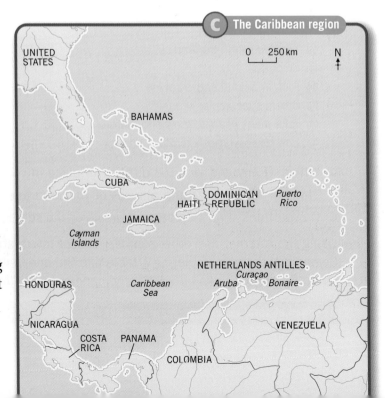

C The Caribbean region

UNITED STATES

0   250 km   N

BAHAMAS

CUBA

HAITI   DOMINICAN REPUBLIC   Puerto Rico

JAMAICA

Cayman Islands

NETHERLANDS ANTILLES
Curaçao
Aruba   Bonaire

HONDURAS

Caribbean Sea

NICARAGUA

COSTA RICA   PANAMA

VENEZUELA

COLOMBIA

Tourist activity		Damage caused
Scuba diving		Divers can damage the delicate coral reef ecosystems.
Snorkelling		Inexperienced snorkellers can trample coral with their flippers, by getting too close or resting on the reef. They often do not realise the damage they cause.
Boat trips		Cruises taking visitors out to the reefs are often careless where they drop anchor.
Boat trips		The water movement caused by boats travelling too fast or too close damages coral reefs.
Boat hire		Tourists do not know the local waters and can run aground on a reef.

D Direct impacts of tourism on coral reef ecosystems

Curaçao

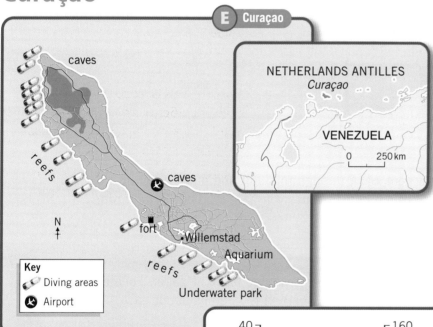

E Curaçao

NETHERLANDS ANTILLES
Curaçao

VENEZUELA

0   250 km

Key
🐚 Diving areas
✈ Airport

caves

reefs

caves

N

fort
•Willemstad
★ Aquarium
reefs
Underwater park

Curaçao may be a tourist paradise, but it is a conservationist's nightmare. Today, few tourists in the Caribbean stop here. But if tourist development is not carefully managed it could become yet another tropical island swamped by hotel chains and wealthy western tourists.

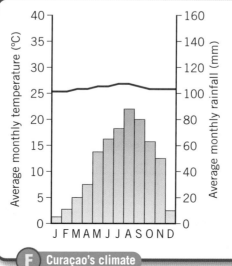

F Curaçao's climate

Activities

1 Imagine that you are planning a holiday to Curaçao. Use the information on these pages and an atlas to help you plan your trip.

  a Describe the location of Curaçao.

  b Use climate graph **F** to write a short description of the climate of Curaçao. Suggest a good time of year to visit the island.

  c Study map **E**. Which part of the island do you think has more tourist development – the east or west coast? Explain your reasons.

  d Write a postcard home describing your time on the island. Accessing the Internet (see **4**) will help you add more detail.

2 Table **D** shows the direct impacts tourists can have on coral reefs. Use the following phrases to produce a similar table showing the indirect impacts tourism may have on coral reefs.

  ◎ Solid waste disposal from cruise boats

  ◎ Pollution from coastal tourism development

  ◎ Overfishing the reefs to feed the increasing number of tourists

  ◎ Local rural people looking for work in the tourist industry set up squatter camps on the coast.

3 Tourists and boat crews damage coral reefs mainly through ignorance. Design an information sheet to explain to tourists visiting Curaçao how and why they should use the reefs carefully. Suggest where it should be displayed.

4 Follow the links at www.heinemann.co.uk/hotlinks (code 5430P) to find out more about Curaçao.

Review and reflect

In this unit you have studied ecosystems, a variety of natural resources and the way people use and misuse them. You have learned that people often have different views and attitudes about resource issues and how to solve them for the future. You may have discovered that, even within your class, students' opinions about resources and the environment can be very different.

The overexploitation of any resource is not a responsible way to manage our global ecosystems. As you have seen in this unit, overfishing of our oceans and seas is creating social, economic and environmental problems. These problems are repeated where any natural resource is being exploited, not just for the current generation but for those in the future too. If we are to show consideration for future generations, then we need to manage natural resources in a more sustainable way.

A We caught him in polluted water

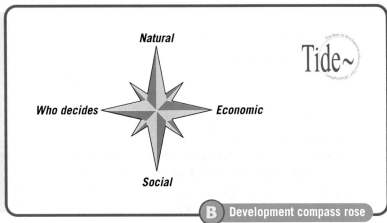

B Development compass rose

Activities

① **a** Work in pairs or small groups. Look back through this unit and make a list in rough of all the resource and environmental issues you have studied. Write down:

- what the issue is
- where the examples are located
- a few key points about the issue.

b Stick an outline map of the world in the centre of a large piece of paper. Locate all the issues on the map, then neatly annotate (label) on the details about each.

c Discuss which issues:

- have already had an effect on your lives
- might affect young people in other parts of the world
- might affect young people in future.

d Find a way of showing your ideas on your map.

② Choose one resource or environmental issue from this unit to think about in depth.

a Make a copy of the development compass rose **B** in the centre of a large piece of paper.

b In pairs, discuss the issue, then write around the outside which problems or changes are:

- **N**atural – to do with ecosystems
- **E**conomic – to do with jobs and money
- **S**ocial – to do with people and the way they live
- **W**ho decides – the people who make decisions.

③ Look at cartoon **A** above. In pairs, discuss what you think it is saying about the global future.

Glossary

Active zone   An area where two tectonic plates meet. Earthquakes and volcanoes occur in active zones.

Adaptations   special features developed by plants to help them survive in an environment, e.g. extreme hot and dry conditions.

Aid   Help that is given by one country to another, either after an emergency such as an earthquake or to help to improve living standards.

Altitude   height of the land above sea level.

Anticyclone   A high-pressure weather system that brings settled weather, hot in summer, cold in winter.

Arch   a natural rock bridge formed when the sea erodes through a headland.

Atmosphere   the layer of gases surrounding the Earth.

Cave   a hole beneath the surface or in a cliff formed by the action of water.

Central Business District (CBD)   The area of a city where there are many shops and offices.

Chalk   a hard, white sedimentary rock made up of the skeletons of millions of tiny sea animals.

Cirrus   high-level cloud formed of ice crystals.

Clay   a soft, fine sedimentary rock.

Climate   The average weather conditions of a place or region measured over many years.

Conflict   where groups of people have different ideas about how an area should be used. These conflicts can be shown on a **conflict matrix**.

Confluence   The place where two or more streams or rivers join.

Convection rain   heavy rain formed by the cooling of moist air which has risen from the heated ground or sea.

Core   Very hot rocks in the centre of the Earth.

Crude oil   petroleum in its natural liquid state as it emerges from the ground, before refining.

Crust   The thin outer layer of the Earth.

Cumulonimbus   very tall storm clouds formed when air rises very quickly.

Cumulus   heaped up masses of cloud with bumpy tops.

Deposition   when a river or the sea dumps or **deposits** what it is carrying.

Depression   A low-weather pressure system that brings changeable weather, often rain, cloud and wind.

Development aid   Aid that is given to help a country to improve its living standards so that it can progress.

Diet   The usual food that people eat.

Discharge   the volume of water which passes through a river at one point in time, measured in cubic metres per second.

Donor   A country that gives aid to another country.

Drainage basin   The area of land drained by a river.

Drought   a period of low rainfall, often over many years.

Earthquake   Shaking and vibration of the ground caused by movements of the Earth's crust.

Economic asset   Something or somebody that makes money for a family or a country, for example, children in LEDCs who work to boost their family's income.

Economic burden   Something or somebody that costs a family or a country money, for example, children who are too young to work.

Emergency relief aid   Aid that is given to help solve the problems caused by a disaster such as an earthquake or flooding.

Enquiry   Geographers carry out an enquiry or investigation to find out about people and places.

Epicentre   The point on the ground above the focus of an earthquake where the vibration is greatest.

Equator   An imaginary line round the middle of the Earth which represents the 00° line of latitude.

Eruption   When a volcano erupts, magma from inside the Earth escapes to the surface.

Evacuate   Take people from a place that is dangerous because of, for example, floods or an earthquake, to a safer place.

Evaluation   Looking at something to see how well done or useful it is by looking at its strengths and weaknesses.

Evapotranspiration   the total loss of water by evaporation from the soil and other surfaces plus water released from plants.

Factor   One of the reasons for something.

Favela   Brazilian for shanty town.

Focus   The focus of an earthquake is the point under the ground that the shock waves travel out from.

Food chain   a cycle that begins with green plants that take their energy from sunlight, continuing with organisms that eat these plants, to other organisms that consume the plant-eating organisms, then to decomposers that break down the dead bodies of those organisms so that they can be used as soil nutrients by plants, starting the cycle again.

Forecast   a weather forecast is a prediction of future weather using scientific evidence.

Foreshocks   Small earthquake shocks which come before the main earthquake. They can help warn people of a coming earthquake.

Front   When warm and cold air masses meet, the boundary is called a front.

Frontal rain   precipitation caused when warm air is forced to rise over cooler air.

Geothermal energy   Heat energy from the Earth that can be used to generate electricity.

Gradient   slope.

Granite   a very hard igneous rock made of crystals of minerals.

Headlands   hard rocks which are left jutting out into the sea, often as cliffs.

Hydrological cycle   a never-ending circulation of water: water evaporates from the sea and land, rises and condenses to form clouds. It then falls back to Earth as precipitation.

Hypothesis   A theory about something that can be tested by an enquiry.

Informal work   Work which does not have a regular wage, and where the worker does not pay taxes.

In-migration   The movement of people into a place.

Inoculate   To protect someone from a disease by giving them a pill or injection containing a minute amount of the organism that causes it.

Irrigate   To transport water to an area where there is a shortage, usually for growing crops.

Isotherm   a line on a map that joins places with the same temperature.

Labour   The workforce of a country or place.

Lava   Liquid rock that flows down the sides of a volcano.

Less Economically Developed Country (LEDC)   A country with a poor economy where many people live in rural areas.

Location   The position of a place or other feature.

Longshore drift   the transport of material along a beach. It happens when waves hit the beach at an angle.

Magma   Molten rock from beneath the surface of the Earth that escapes to the surface when a volcano erupts. It appears as liquid lava, volcanic bombs, ash, dust, steam and gases.

Mainshock   The biggest shock of an earthquake.

Mantle   The layer of hot, molten rock that comes between the Earth's crust and its core.

Marble   a hard metamorphic rock.

Meteorologist   a scientist who studies the weather.

Minutes   Latitude and longitude are measured in degrees and minutes. There are 60 minutes in a degree.

Monitoring   Making measurements at regular intervals to see if there are any changes. In earthquake areas, for example, scientists use seismographs to detect the first signs of ground movement.

More Economically Developed Country (MEDC)   A country with a wealthy economy where a high percentage of people live in urban areas.

Official aid   Aid that is given by a government and paid for by its taxpayers.

Out-migration   The movement of people out of a place.

Ozone layer   the layer of the upper atmosphere, from about 12 to 50 kilometres above the Earth's surface, that protects the Earth from harmful radiation from the Sun.

Permanent settlement   A place where people live throughout the year, such as a housing estate.

Photosynthesis   green plants use the energy of sunlight to convert carbon dioxide and water into energy which they use for growth. At the same time they release oxygen into the air.

Population density   The number of people per area of land. This is **high** when many people live in a place, or **low** where only a few people live.

Population pyramid   A type of bar chart that shows the population structure of a country. Because the number of babies goes at the bottom of the chart and the number of very old people at the top, the chart often looks like a pyramid.

Population structure   The age groups that make up the population of a country.

Prediction   Estimating what is going to happen in the future.

Primary productivity   the rate at which green plants, store energy as carbohydrates to be consumed by other organisms.

Recipient   A country that receives aid from another country.

Refined oil   oil in a form that can be used in, for example, homes and cars. It is made by removing the impurities from crude oil.

Relief   The shape of an area of land – whether it is flat, hilly or mountainous.

Relief rain   precipitation caused when air is forced to rise over hills and mountains.

Satellite image   A photograph of part of the Earth's surface taken from a satellite in space.

Seismograph   An instrument that measures the shaking of the ground to give the magnitude of an earthquake. It records the vibrations on a graph called a seismogram.

Self-build housing   Houses built by the people who are going to live in them, for example in shanty towns.

Settlement   A place where people live. It may be just a few homes or a large city.

Shanty town   A squatter settlement, often on the outskirts of a city, built by people on land that does not belong to them.

Shock waves   Shock waves travel out from the focus of an earthquake into the surrounding area, making the ground vibrate.

Site   The exact location of a settlement. This often includes the physical features of the place it is built on, such as whether it is by a river.

Situation   The broader picture of where a place is. A settlement's situation can be described by looking at an atlas.

Sparsely populated   An area with a low population density, i.e. few people live there.

Spit   a long beach formed by longshore drift. Spits often stretch across the mouths of rivers or where the coast suddenly changes direction.

Stable population   A population that is not getting larger or smaller because the death rate and the birth rate are the same.

Stack   the remains of collapsed arches left when a clffline retreats.

Stratus   low clouds forming a layer or 'sheet' across the sky.

Sustainability   the wise use of resources today, so that people in the future can still use them. Resources used in this way are **sustainable**.

Symbol   A sign or emblem that is used to represent something, such as a symbol on a map. A map has a key to show what each symbol means.

Synoptic chart   A map that shows the areas of high and low pressure in a region at a particular time.

Tectonic plates   The Earth's crust is made up of huge slabs called tectonic plates.

Temperate   A climate, like that one of the British Isles, that is neither very hot nor very cold is temperate.

Temporary settlement   A place where people live for a short time, such as a nomad encampment or an oil rig.

Transnational   A transnational company does business all over the world.

Transport   carry; for example, rock fragments that have been eroded are removed or transported by the sea, wind, ice or rivers.

Tributary   A river that flows into a larger river.

UNICEF   United Nations Children's Fund.

Vegetation   The plants in a particular area.

Velocity   the speed of a river, calculated in metres per second.

Vent   The opening in a volcano where molten rock escapes to the surface.

Volcanic bombs   Lumps of molten rock that solidify as they fall from the sky during a volcanic eruption.

Volcano   An opening in the Earth's crust where molten rock from inside the Earth is able to escape to the surface.

Voluntary aid   Aid that is given by individuals through charities such as the Red Cross.

Water cycle   A continuous process in which water falls to Earth from the air as precipitation, evaporates and condenses to form clouds, and falls back to Earth again.

Water vapour   water when it is a gas.

Weather   The conditions of the atmosphere, such as the temperature, amount of rain or hours of sunshine.

Weather system   An anticyclone or a depression.

Weathering   the breakdown of rocks due to exposure to air, moisture and plants and animals.

Index